USING SCRIPTURE IN PASTORAL COUNSELING

USING SCRIPTURE in PASTORAL COUNSELING

Edward P. Wimberly

Abingdon Press
Nashville

USING SCRIPTURE IN PASTORAL COUNSELING

Copyright © 1994 by Abingdon Press

This book is printed on acid-free, recycled paper.

Scripture quotations, except for brief paraphrases, or unless otherwise noted, are from The New Revised Standard Version Bible, copyright © 1989, by the Division of Christian Education of the National Council of the Churches of Christ in the United States of America. Used by permission.

Those noted RSV are from the Revised Standard Version of the Bible, copyright 1946, 1952, 1971 by the Division of Christian Education of the National Council of Churches of Christ in the U.S.A. Used by permission.

Those noted KJV are from the King James or Authorized version of the Bible.

Library of Congress Cataloging-in-Publication Data

Wimberly, Edward P., 1943–
    Using Scripture in pastoral counseling / Edward P. Wimberly
      p. cm.
    Includes bibliographical references.
    ISBN 0-687-00251-6 (pbk. : alk. paper)
     1. Pastoral counseling.   2. Bible—Use.   I. Title.
    BV4012.2.W494   1993
    253.5—dc20   93-28847
                                        CIP

94 95 96 97 98 99 00 01 02 03 —10 9 8 7 6 5 4 3 2 1

MANUFACTURED IN THE UNITED STATES OF AMERICA

CONTENTS

ACKNOWLEDGMENTS

The Interdenominational Theological Center in Atlanta, Georgia, through its Status, Tenure, and Welfare Committee, provided financial assistance that was necessary to bring this manuscript to full completion. Abingdon Press through Ulrike Guthrie provided the necessary editorial assistance that enabled the manuscript to become a book.

In addition to the institutional support, many individuals provided support through reading and making valuable critical comments on the manuscript so that it could reach publication. Among these persons were William Harris, Flora Bridges, Normal Phillips, Willie and Delores Johnson, Mary Ann Milhone, Rita Bigham, and Suzanne Grier-Bowman.

There were also several colleagues who gave encouragement and read the manuscript. These persons included Carolyn McCrary, Wayne Merritt, Thomas J. Pugh, Robert Jewett, Richard Stegner, and John Patton.

My gratitude to these people is immense.

T his book presents a model for using Scripture in pastoral counseling. It outlines steps to be taken with counselees who come from biblically rich church traditions and who use the Bible as a primary means of giving expression to their experience and feelings. Very little attention is given to counselees who do not use the Bible as a fundamental tool for articulating their experience. Nor is attention given to those persons who find themselves in churches without a fruitful and plentiful storytelling tradition. However, several things can be said to pastoral counselors who desire to use Bible stories with counselees who have very little background with the Bible.

In my book *African American Pastoral Care,* I explore the use of stories that spontaneously come to the minds and hearts of pastoral counselors as they interact with their counselees.[1] Such stories arise from imaginative intuition or empathy, which generates the story-making process within the pastoral counselor as a response to the needs of the counselee. Part of in-depth pastoral counseling is trusting what is stirring within one's intuition that results from interaction with the counselee. Often these stirrings are related to the so-called contagion or contagious therapeutic ideas, which go to the heart of the needs of the counselees. Although such intuitive stirrings form within the pastoral counselor, the actual source of the therapeutic idea is the psychological life of the counselee. The pastoral counseling interaction simply acts as a trigger that allows the idea to germinate.

Often the communication between the pastoral counselor and the counselee suggests within the pastoral counselor a biblical story. When the pastoral counselor trusts his or her own intuition, he or she can risk sharing with the counselee the Bible stories that result. Sharing such stories may be all that is needed to strike a chord within the counselee that will lead to a fruitful therapeutic session.

The point is that pastoral counselors need to trust the contagion process of story generation. They need to learn to share these stories without fearing they will contaminate the pastoral counseling session or transgress the boundary of respect for the counselee. However, the pastoral counselor should always check to be sure that it is all right to share, that the timing is right and that the person is ready to hear the story. If the story is contagion-generated, the counselee will welcome the input without feeling that something is being imposed on him or her. Getting permission to share the story contributes to respecting the counselee's right not to have the pastoral counselor's stories imposed.

Counselor-generated stories that are truly the result of the contagion process in pastoral counseling are central to using the Bible in pastoral counseling. If the timing is right and the story is truly contagious, the Bible story begins to enter the pastoral counseling in transformative ways.

A BIBLICAL NARRATIVE MODEL FOR PASTORAL COUNSELING

Again, the concern in this book is with counselees who come from Bible-rich traditions and who use Bible stories as a basic means of bringing meaning to their lives. The model presented in these pages has seven dimensions, which can be summarized briefly as: (1) Attending to the presenting problem; (2) attending to the mythology, whether personal, marital, or family; (3) identifying the nature of the mythology; (4) mapping the influence of the mythology; (5) attending to the preferred story; (6) setting goals; and (7) re-authoring the mythology.

Step 1 in the model addresses the story surrounding the presenting problem, or initial concern that led to the need for counseling. It is important to ascertain information from the counselee about his or her history of personal family relationships, education, health, vocation, sexual relationships, and religion as these relate to the presenting problem. Especially important in this phase of the counseling is the religious history, which can help the pastoral counselor get a feel for how counselees use religious resources and language in everyday life. Attention needs to be given as well to the role-taking ability of counselees.

Step 2 involves attending to the personal, marital, or family mythology that surrounds the presenting problem. Here the concern is for the convictions, beliefs, and themes that make up the personal, marital, and family mythology.

Step 3 involves identifying the personal, marital, and family mythologies at work in the counselee and calling them to attention.

Step 4 maps with the counselee or counselees the actual impact of the mythologies on their lives. Attention is given to how the mythologies have informed the counselees' responses to presenting problems and to other problems of life.

Step 5 helps the counselee discern a preferred story for his or her life. Bible stories with which the counselee identifies can be used to facilitate the discernment. At this stage, the pastoral counselor can also give attention to contagion-generated stories if they surface.

Step 6 sets goals based on the preferred story that need to be enacted in the lives of the counselees.

Step 7 begins the actual re-authoring or modifying of the stories that dominate and frustrate the counselee's life. Attention needs to be given to how the drawing power of Bible stories and the identification with Bible stories are affecting the re-authoring effort.

The goal of employing this methodology is to transform the life of the counselee and to help link the counselee to resources—namely, Bible stories—that can assist in the transformation.

Three Vignettes

Pastoral counselors have long argued about whether use of Scripture is appropriate in their work with counselees. In my own experience, I have found it a particularly helpful resource. For this reason I want to reflect on the how and why of incorporating biblical material in counseling. Three cases are to be explored in depth to illustrate how I have used the Bible in pastoral counseling. A brief vignette of each serves here to introduce them.

RESTIN

The first vignette is of Restin, a forty-nine-year-old male with a long history of substance abuse. Growing up in a Pentecostal denomination, he was taught from early childhood that God answers prayers of those in distress. In early childhood he also became fascinated with Bible stories and biblical characters. By the time he was a teenager, he had read most of the Bible and knew a significant number of its stories.

Despite Restin's familiarity with the Bible, he always felt that he was outside the influence and healing power of the gospel. Because of his substance abuse, he experienced Bible stories and the characters in them as a world from which he was excluded, except for his identification with the pathetic and unfortunate characters and stories. Because of some "not good enough" family relationships, he believed that there was something inherently wrong with him. He felt like he was forever doomed to remain outside the embrace of salvation. Despite his pessimistic forecast, he desperately wanted to be part of God's salvation and healing.

Restin was intrigued by the idea that he might be included in God's salvation drama. In fact, he recalled a short period in his life when he had experienced inclusion within God's household. However, this short period of inclusion was followed by a longer period of disappointment and disillusion with the church and its gospel after the death of his brother from cancer. Following the loss of his brother, he felt completely alienated from God. The old feelings of being excluded and inherently flawed returned to dominate his life.

JOAN

A young woman named Joan was returning home from a Bible study group late one night. At a red light a man broke into her car, kidnapped her, and then raped her. He locked her in the trunk, and later burned up her car thinking that she would be burned up inside it.

Joan had found a way to escape from the locked trunk without being detected. She found help, and her needs were tended by the police and medical personnel. Several days after the terrible event she sought me out for pastoral counseling.

Since a child in Sunday school, Joan had learned to interpret her experiences in the light of Bible stories. She developed the idea that what happened to her could be somehow dealt with from the perspective of God's love and goodness. She identified with biblical characters who encountered hardship in life, but she also believed that her life would eventually turn out in a positive way, as had the lives of some of the main biblical characters. She learned to view her life as an unfolding drama that was leading toward a purposeful end. Consequently, when she was raped, she was able to see her life apart from the one harrowing experience as still having meaning, value, and purpose. Moreover, she saw her escape from death as a miracle wrought by God. The actual rape was viewed as Satan's work to distract her from her vocation in ministry.

Joan's religious faith and personal tendency to interpret her life in terms of biblical faith and characters served her well in overcoming the tragic rape. Based on my work with her and the second opinion of a psychiatrist who interviewed her, it was concluded she had not suffered any lasting negative emotional and psychological harm from the rape. This was in large part due to her way of viewing life from a biblical perspective, her support system in her local church, and pastoral counseling.

DELORES, WILL, AND THEIR CHILDREN

Delores and her husband, Will, suffered the bathtub drowning death of their second child as the result of a tragic mistake that was interpreted as negligence by Delores. Following two years of pastoral counseling, Delores and Will were able to face realistically the tragic event, and they chronicled the role the Bible had played in their recovery. Delores found her faith in God and the role of the Bible especially central to her recovery. The Bible helped her face her guilt and find forgiveness in God. Now she and Will are fully involved in their ministries free from bondage to a tragic event in their lives.

HOW SCRIPTURE CAN HELP

This book will be of interest to those pastors and pastoral counselors who desire to use religious resources, namely the Bible, in a narrative scriptural model of pastoral counseling focused on counselor facilitation and counselees' self-growth. This book seeks to distinguish between a nongrowth-authoritarian use of Scripture and a growth-facilitative-authoritative use of Scripture. Authoritarian uses of Scripture seek to make children of counselees and to frustrate the growth of persons toward their full possibilities as human beings. Authoritative uses of Scripture aim to appropriate those dimensions of Scripture that support the empowering of humans to become full and responsible participants in life. What follows in these pages is what I have learned about the use of Scripture in pastoral counseling to facilitate such growth.

My belief that the Bible can be used to facilitate growth is influenced by the faith community in which I grew up. Because I am African American and grew up in a Christian environment where Bible stories were normative for making sense out of life, I have storied my life using Bible stories since I was a child. "Storying" refers to organizing human experience using stories. Through my own personal therapy, I have come to realize that the relationships with significant others as a child influenced significantly how Bible stories functioned in my life. I have also come to realize that Bible stories with which I identified as a child functioned to bring healing and wholeness in my life despite some of the negative convictions that I had about myself. The more I addressed the negative perceptions I had of myself through therapy, the more I could discern the role that Bible stories had in shaping my positive sense of self. This realization has helped me to help those Christian counselees who believe that the Bible has normative significance in their lives to discern the positive role of Bible stories in their personal growth.

My approach to using the Bible in pastoral counseling has also been shaped by my pastoral counseling experience. Most of my pastoral counseling load consists of African American Christians whose lives have been influenced in both positive and negative ways by the church and the Bible. This has also been true for non–African American Christians with whom I have counseled over the years. In this sense this book addresses a cross-cultural Christian audience which feels that the Bible has some normative relevance in their lives.

CHAPTER ONE

A MODEL FOR USING SCRIPTURE IN PASTORAL COUNSELING

A model is a design or pattern that is used to guide some activity. In this chapter a model is presented of the various steps I take in pastoral counseling with biblically oriented and familiarized counselees. Case materials are introduced initially to lay an experiential foundation for the model.

Restin was introduced in the first vignette. He came to counseling seeking help in overcoming his self-destructive behavior with drug abuse. He said, "I can see that the road I was on was leading to destruction and death." He saw death as an end to his present difficulty, but he recognized that life was still worth living. His chief complaint, however, was that his wife did not believe anything he said and that she did not recognize the damage that this was doing to his self-worth.

The context of the problem was a recent incident: He had sold his wedding ring to buy cocaine. His wife was very angry and was threatening to leave if he did not seek help with his drug problem and get personal counseling.

At the time of the counseling he was forty-nine years of age. He was unemployed and relied on his wife's job and money to survive. They had been married for more than twenty years, during which she took most of the financial burden on herself.

He did hold down jobs during this time, but he had an inconsistent work record.

He had one living brother and three living sisters. One brother nearest his age had died of cancer in his mid thirties. Restin was the fourth child born. His father was dead, and his mother was eighty years of age at the time of the counseling. He described his parents as very poor. His father had had very little education. His mother had worked outside the home but with very little education and limited job skills. His parents had been churchgoers and believed in God.

Restin described his parents as disciplinarians who believed that sparing the rod spoiled the child. He said, their children "were not spoiled." Restin had a nightly problem with bed-wetting for which he was beaten. His parents took him to the doctor, who could find no cause for the bed-wetting. The doctor told his father to treat him like a dog, by rubbing his nose in his urine. Restin said his father tried this with no success, and Restin felt hurt that his father treated him literally like a dog. He also felt that he was the scapegoat of the family and as a result was not able to do well in school. He would wet his pants in school, and therefore further hated school. His parents' response to his bed-wetting led to his having very little confidence in himself.

This background set the stage for his problems in life. He had very high self-expectations and continued to punish himself because he had made nothing of himself. He looked to his wife to take care of him and make up for his miserable childhood and adolescence.

Restin's personal convictions and beliefs included a feeling of not really being wanted by his parents. He felt as if he was a burden to them since they were poor and had very few financial resources. Named after a grandfather on his mother's side, he was the fourth child but the first boy to be born. His mother had very high expectations for Restin and wanted him to be what neither she nor his father could be. Restin said his mother was consequently very disappointed in his bed-wetting and at his inability to do well in school.

From the very beginning of counseling, Restin identified with Bible stories. He brought with him a history of biblical role-taking—identifying with Bible stories and taking on the role of its characters. He said that he was a believer and had always found religion to be of interest. The stories of the children of Israel in the wilderness, the Gerasene demoniac, and Jonah were of special interest to him at the time of counseling. He entertained the idea that God would eventually love him, but he felt that God could not possibly love him in his current condition.

The goal he had for counseling was to exorcise the ghosts of the past that were defeating him. I identified the center of his problem as addictive behavior rooted in a defective core self. He had unrealistic self-expectations, and he internalized punitive introjects that constantly put him down and sabotaged his efforts to grow. He needed to enter into drug treatment, and his wife needed to attend a program for addictive spouses because of being a co-dependent. This would benefit both of them, for Restin knew that as things stood she would take care of him and that he did not have to care for himself.

This is a brief description of the presenting problem and the ingredients that made up Restin's personal mythology. Once this information was gathered, I began to try to map how this picture had influenced his life.

Restin's personal mythology (self-convictions and beliefs) was rooted in the themes of scapegoat, black sheep of the family, bed-wetter, being possessed by the devil, a God who loved only those who deserved love, and being a disappointment to others. Other themes (discussed in a later chapter) include entitlement, triumphalism, and wilderness. Undergirding these themes were negative experiences with significant others in his life, which were the source of his defective self-image. Restin had deep distaste for himself. He felt greatly wounded in his life and sought to soothe his defective self through drugs and alcohol. He did not identify any particular secular story that he liked, but it was obvious that the themes indicated a losing script undergirding his life. If I had to characterize his script, I would call it tragic, and it was one that he reenacted continually. His personal mythology reminded me of the Greek myth of Sisyphus, who was condemned to continually roll a stone up a hill only to have the stone roll back down the hill before it could be pushed over the hill. Restin was also rolling stones uphill and getting nowhere.

The impact of this personal mythology on his life was devastating. He had a cocaine and alcohol problem, he engaged in self-defeating behavior on the job and in his marriage, he had no real control over his life, and he was very irresponsible.

The most difficult problem Restin faced was that he believed he was possessed by the devil. He said that he felt he had literally encountered Satan as a child. When he had run to tell his mother, she laughed at him and said he must have looked in the mirror. From then on, he felt as if the destructive force in him was supernatural. He felt that he could not become responsible and overcome drug addiction and alcohol addiction without divine help. He was very reluctant to seek psychological help and drug treatment because he believed that his problem had spiritual roots. Even when he came for counseling, he resisted supplementing the counseling with drug treatment.

Restin's belief that he was possessed by the devil led him to identify with the Gerasene demoniac when he first heard the story as a child. His feeling of rejection by his parents, his sense of encountering the devil in his life, and his mother's pointing to him as Satan confirmed in his own mind that he was Satan. His religious teaching about Satan and the destructive work that Satan did led him to develop, believe in, and act out a destructive personal mythology. Consequently, his role-taking penchant led him to a story that confirmed his negative feelings about himself. However, the power of the story itself was at work in him seeking to draw him deeper into the story so that he could experience healing and wholeness.

Although the prognosis for counseling looked bleak, there were some spiritual resources in the form of Bible stories that were at work in him. The New Testament story of the Gerasene demoniac and the Old Testament stories of the children of Israel in the wilderness and the experience of Jonah were all at work in him. Somehow they held a fascination for him. Somehow—I thought—their power could bring him to wholeness. In these stories I saw possible new stories around which he could organize his life. These stories held out potential for re-authoring his tragic personal mythology. Consequently, our goal became to learn to follow the lead of the Scripture at work in his life as it tried to challenge and confront his personal mythology.

This case illustration is a good introduction to the narrative model of using the Bible in pastoral counseling. It is a case involving a person who is biblically oriented and who derives a significant part of his meaning in life from Bible stories. Because this orientation presented itself very early in pastoral counseling, I decided to make it an important thrust of my pastoral counseling with the counselee. Below is a general outline of the model, which was operative in parts of the case.

THE BIBLICAL NARRATIVE MODEL

All pastoral counseling begins with the presenting problem that individuals, marital partners, and families bring to pastoral counseling. The problem usually unfolds like a story, in dramatic fashion one scene at a time. Consequently, I spend the early stages of counseling attending to the presenting problem and the story that surrounds the problem. Once I have heard the story related to the presenting problem, I make an attempt to gain insight into how this story has developed over time and how it is related to the counselee's personal history, family history, relationship history, and other factors like education, health, vocation, and sexual functioning.

After the presenting problem and related data have been explored, I begin to try to put together a picture of the counselee's self-beliefs and self-conviction. The self-beliefs and convictions are called one's personal mythology. A personal mythology is made up of the symbolic and emotionally laden themes that make up the self and the self-in-relation-to-others, which includes the internalized ideas of significant others.[1] The purpose of attending to the personal mythology of the counselee is to discern how the stories that undergird the counselee's life contribute to the presenting problem. Often the presenting problem is accompanied by a personal mythology that makes it difficult for the counselee to address the problem-saturated dimensions of his or her life.

Identifying the Personal Mythology

Discerning the personal mythology undergirding the presenting problem involves several steps.[2] First, I raise questions about the earliest memory the counselee has about his or her family of origin. This helps reveal the theme or themes that concern the counselee right now. The next exploration is what I call the examination of the birth mythology of the counselee. This mythology concerns the stories the counselee heard about his or her conception, time in the womb, and the early weeks of his or her life. The following questions can help reveal the birth mythology of the counselee: (1) What circumstances, beliefs, and values do you think played a role in your parents' decision to have you? (2) What do you think your mother's and father's reactions were after seeing you for the first time? (3) What were the reactions of your parents and siblings on discovering that your mother was pregnant with you? Such questions often get to the foundations of the personal myth in that they help to reveal the welcome the child gets to the world.

Other areas of investigation include parental feelings about the counselee's gender, the naming process, and the nicknaming process. These areas help to ascertain the prescribed behaviors and roles assigned to the counselee. Parental expectations for the counselee are also key areas of evaluation along with discovering the actual role the counselee played in the family.

Personal mythology also involves the favorite fairy tale, book, short story, play, movie, or television show that the counselee has. The story chosen usually contains the core conflicts, themes, and roles that are prevalent in the counselee's life. When examining this narrative area, it is also important to raise similar questions about the Bible stories with which the counselee identifies. This is important because the pastoral counselor is interested in the influence of the Bible on the life of the counselee.

Exploration of a person's image of God is also crucial in revealing personal mythology. The image of God as authoritarian judge, as distant observer, or as caring presence each holds potential for discovering themes of the personal mythology.

Questioning in all of these areas can reveal a great deal about the narrative picture the counselee holds. After the pastoral counselor has examined the personal mythology, the next step is to help the counselee discern the relationship between the personal mythology and the presenting problem.

Mapping the Influence of the Personal Mythology

Once the personal mythology has been identified with all of its related themes, it is important to trace the influence of the personal mythology on the counselee's life.[3] This includes the presenting problem, but it also goes beyond the presenting problem. A counselee needs to visualize the way the personal mythology has dominated his or her life, and how this story has shaped responses to a variety of situations in life. Emphasis needs to be placed on the fact that any significant changes that take place in the counselee's life will take place largely because he or she has given some attention to the personal mythology.

Attending to the Preferred Story

Once the pastoral counselor and the counselee have identified the personal mythology and its themes, and mapped its influence, the task is to address the preferred story that the counselee would like to see lived out in his or her life. Here the attention needs to be focused on the presenting problem and what the counselee hopes will result from pastoral counseling.

Part of attending to the preferred story means exploring the role that the Bible might have in helping the counselee design and enact the preferred story. Here the pastoral counselor engages the counselee in a discussion of the significant Bible stories that have surfaced in the early stages of pastoral counseling. The aim of the discussion is to (1) compare the preferred story and the Bible story, and (2) to get a glimpse of how the Bible story is at work within the counselee to assist in developing the preferred story.

Setting Goals

Once the preferred scenario or narrative has been identified and the relationship of the Bible to it, the next step involves enacting the preferred story. This step largely consists of exploring the areas of the person's life and story that will be the focus of counseling. Once these areas have been identified, goals are set and the process of re-authoring the personal mythology and dealing with the presenting problem begins.

Re-authoring

Re-authoring refers to the process of modifying one's personal mythology through the process of pastoral counseling. This re-authoring begins as soon as counseling starts. However, early re-authoring is largely outside the awareness of the counselee. Not until goals are set to achieve the preferred story does re-authoring become a conscious effort.

In the re-authoring phase, the use of Bible stories is extremely important. The first step in using the Bible is to reintroduce the story into the counseling process. During the early stages of the pastoral counseling, a particular Bible story or stories were identified. Their potential role in counseling was also recognized. At this point the actual role of the Bible story for re-authoring the personal mythology begins to take shape.

Once the Bible story is introduced in the re-authoring stage, the pastoral counselor employs the methods of similarity and identification, methods of exploring the drawing power of story, and methods of discerning expectation and challenge. All of these methods are narrative methods of counseling that I have found helpful in exploring the use of the Bible in pastoral counseling.

Similarity and identification refer to the ability of the counselee to take the role of the main characters in the Bible story.[4] Identification with the Bible story and character is made based on the similarity of the counselee's life situation and the situation of the Bible story. Often this identification is made with the pain that one or more of the Bible characters has in his or her life. The point is that the counselee often visualizes himself or herself as one of the biblical characters in one of the stories.

Identification with particular Bible stories and characters is often related to the drawing power of the Bible story and character itself. That is, some biblical narrative critics say that the Bible story has the power to draw readers and hearers into the story based on the story's own narrative power.[5] Biblical stories often contain an invitation to the reader to adopt the perspective, feelings, and attitudes of the characters as a way to influence the life of the reader and hearer. The role of the pastoral counselor in this exploration of the drawing power of the Bible story is to discern whether there are some narrative forces at work on the counselee because of identification with the story. The significance of this step is to call to the counselee's awareness that something is at work in the depths of his or her being.

Closely related to exploring the drawing power of the Bible story is the method of examining the expectation and facilitating the challenge. In both biblical narrative criticism and role theory there is a process known as expectation. Expectation refers to the fact that people who identify with biblical stories often expect their lives to be influenced in ways similar to those of the characters in the Bible story.[6] It is important that the pastoral counselor examine whether the counselee's identification with the Bible story has actually grown into an expectation that his or her life would have similar "outcomes" as the lives of biblical characters.

Attending to the expectations of the counselee who is familiar with the Bible often leads to a challenge to the personal mythology of the counselee. The drawing power of the story and its characters leads to a certain expectation, and this expectation often challenges the actual negative personal mythology that the counselee has brought to pastoral counseling. The role of the pastoral counselor is to bring this narrative challenge to the awareness of the counselee. The hope of making the counselee aware of this challenge is one of soliciting the counselee's cooperation with what the narrative story is doing.

When using the methods of similarity, identification, expectation, and challenge, I often lean on biblical narrative criticism to inform me in how the narrative draws. Often I read narrative scholars who address concerns about who was in the original audience and the possible impact the narrative might have had on that audience.[7] I then attempt to discern the impact that the Bible story might actually have had on the counselee based on the similarity between the counselee and the original reader or hearer of the story. Such study helps me employ these various re-authoring methods.

Re-authoring is employed throughout the enactment of the preferred story in pastoral counseling. All the psychological counseling skills are employed along with the re-authoring methods to make sure that the relational dimensions of pastoral counseling remain central. The relationship skills of counseling psychology facilitate the re-authoring process in pastoral counseling.

Re-authoring and Marital and Family Mythologies

The emphasis so far has been on personal mythologies. In addition to personal mythologies there are marital and family mythologies.[8] Marital mythologies are built around the expectations that each spouse brings into the marriage partnership regarding the ideal mate.[9] The marital myth is formed based on entering the ideal mate images into dialogue with the actual mate. Family mythologies relate to the images of the ideal family and of the ideal child that each spouse brings to the marriage and how they get changed when an actual child is born into the family.[10]

The pastoral counselor uses the narrative model here in much the same way he or she uses it with personal mythology. The difference is that the exploration is conducted for marital therapy or family therapy. The presenting problem must be explored, and there will come a time when marital and family mythologies have to be explored as well. The relationship of these mythologies to the Bible and Bible stories and how they relate to the presenting problem also needs exploration. At the re-authoring phase, following developing the preferred narrative, the Bible stories and characters are reintroduced followed by the appropriate re-authoring methods introduced earlier.

In the next section the first interview with Restin is introduced as a means of illustrating the first phase of the biblical narrative model of pastoral counseling, which explores the presenting problem.

THE FIRST INTERVIEW WITH RESTIN

P.C.: Tell me a little about why you are here.

Restin: I have really messed up my life and my wife's life. I have this problem with cocaine, and I sold my wedding ring. My wife left me once before, and now she is threatening to do it again.

P.C.: You are here to see if there is something you can do about your problem with cocaine. Tell me a little about your struggle with cocaine.

Restin: It is a long story and a painful one. It seems like I have had this difficulty for a long time. I remember that my cocaine habit got really bad when there was this guy at work who really tried to make my life miserable. He was my boss, and he knew I was religious. He was always trying to make me stumble and fall.

P.C.: What do you mean by stumbling and falling?

Restin: He would do little things to irritate me and to see if I could maintain a level head rather than to blow up. I remember I used to write weekly reports for him. He would always try to find something wrong with them to make me feel uncomfortable.

P.C.: How did you respond to him?

Restin: I kept telling my wife that one day I was going to hurt him real bad. I had fantasies of really beating this man up.

P.C.: Does this mean you never mentioned to your boss your feelings?

Restin: I never really did. I just quit the job. I could only take so much.

P.C.: You walked away from the job?

Restin: Yes.

P.C.: How did this make you feel?

Restin: I really was angry with that man. I thought it better to leave than to get in some real trouble if I hurt him.

P.C.: You would rather quit than to get violent?

Restin: I would have rather gotten violent and gotten revenge for what he did to me.

P.C.: Why didn't you?

Restin: Well, I didn't want to give in to my desire for revenge. I wanted to give in badly, but God seemed to have blocked me.

P.C.: God blocked you?

Restin: I kept thinking of the verse "vengeance is mine says the Lord."

P.C.: You would rather quit your job than make God mad at you?

Restin: God is already angry with me.

P.C.: Tell me what you mean.

Restin: Look at my life. I have made shambles of it. There is no way God could like what he sees in me.

P.C.: You feel separated from God.

Restin: Yes. God could not care about me at all. I am sure that God hates me because of the mess I have made of my life.

P.C.: You feel condemned?

Restin: Very much. I feel there is no real hope for me. I know there is no hope for me unless God, somehow, gets over his anger at me and saves me.

P.C: You really don't believe God will do this?

Restin: How could he? Look at what I have done. I think God is going to let me lie in the mess I have created.

P.C.: Are you really that bad?

Restin: My mother said I was.

P.C.: Say more.

Restin: One of the most painful things I remember was when I actually saw Satan when I was small. I actually saw him in the bathroom. This scared me. So I ran to my mother and told her what I had seen. She laughed and said, "You saw Satan all right. You looked in the mirror."

P.C.:   She really hurt you?

Restin: She did. I really feel like I am possessed. I feel like the Gerasene demoniac. I have many demons in me, just like my mother said.

P.C.:   You identify with the Gerasene demoniac. Do you know what happened to him?

Restin: Yes, Jesus delivered him. But, Jesus won't do that for me. I am too far gone.

P.C.:   Yet, you still hope that this might be possible one day. Do you really want to know if God really cares for you?

Restin: If I thought God cared for me, it would really make a difference to me. I could really have hope.

In this initial interview I was attending to the presenting problem. I was trying to discover what the presenting problem was. I briefly explored the history of the problem he presented, and this led to some of his early memories and feelings related to himself, God, and his mother. When he introduced the Bible character, I immediately explored with him the possible role that this story might actually play in his counseling. He seemed to move into the biblical character so easily in telling his story that I wanted to give some attention to it very early in the session. I also wanted to explore his image of God, since that also seemed to be primary in his thinking about his problem, and resources to deal with it.

I emphasize the fact that many of my counselees move very easily into Bible stories and God language. They usually raise religious subjects themselves. I then test how important this is to them early in the counseling in order to discern whether Bible stories and God language might be an important resource for them in counseling. When they are important, I often initiate the exploration of the stories with which my counselees identify. If I discover that Bible stories or God language are not important resources, I usually attend to the language used by the counselee and draw on it in the counseling. Sometimes opportunities to use Bible stories present themselves later in the counseling session. When this occurs, they can still be used to facilitate the counseling.

RELATIONSHIP TO OTHER MODELS

In the area of pastoral counseling there are three models of using the Bible. These methods include the dynamic use of the Bible, the moral instructional use, and what is referred to as the disclosive power of the text.[11] In the dynamic approach, Bible passages are chosen for their relevance to the psychological dynamics in the life of the counselee. Persons who have used this approach include Wayne Oates and Carroll Wise, and the concern is for the way the Bible can inform the psychological problem the counselee has in ways that are consistent with psychology. The moral instructional approach, represented by Jay Adams, is not concerned with being consistent with psychology. Rather, it is concerned with the passages in Scripture that might influence the moral behavior of the counselee that is inconsistent with faith norms. Finally, the disclosive power of the text approach refers to the text's ability to reveal its meaning and in doing so influence the reader and listener. This approach is represented by Donald Capps, who seeks to augment the dynamic approach with the disclosive approach.

Here and in the ensuing chapters, the effort is made to combine the dynamic and disclosive traditions of the use of the Bible in pastoral care and counseling. The traditional moral instructional approach functions at its best as a rationalistic and cognitive application of theological principles to human behavior. Such a moral and instructional approach used in pastoral counseling can deteriorate into restrictive and rejection-oriented counseling in the hands of a counselor who is not self-aware and psychologically aware. The disclosive approach, on the other hand, focuses somewhat on the moral, rational, and cognitive dimensions, but its primary focus is on the interaction between the counselee or counselees, the pastoral counselor, and the Bible story in question. This approach is inherently dynamic, taking on the logic of narrative drama with emphasis on plots unfolding one scene at a time. It is not limited to the application of the linear logic of rational cognitive therapy. The disclosive approach lends itself to the actual dynamic activity of the Scripture itself within the counselee.

CHAPTER TWO

PERSONAL MYTHOLOGY
AND BIBLE STORIES

In chapter 1, the biblical narrative model for using the Bible in pastoral counseling was presented. Restin's case was introduced to illustrate the initial stage of the model, attending to the presenting problem. This chapter will explore the remaining six stages of the model.

ATTENDING TO PERSONAL MYTHOLOGY

Following is a verbatim report of the second session with Restin, which lifts up and explores issues surrounding his personal mythology.

P.C.:   In our first interview together you raised the issue that God would not save you from your predicament.

Restin: I remember that. I also remember that you indicated that I needed to ask God where he was in my life.

P.C.:   What did you find out?

Restin: You said that when I prayed again, ask God to let me know where he was involved in my life.

P.C.:   Did you?

Restin: I sure did.

P.C.:   What did God tell you?

Restin: Later in the week after I prayed, an insight came to me. All of a sudden a thought came to me to look at my life now and compare it with the way it was last year this time. I discovered that I am much better off this year than last year. I was far worse then than now.

P.C.:   Does this mean you can see God at work in your life?

Restin: Somewhat. I am still disappointed in God, however.

P.C.:   Say more.

Restin: Although I am better off now, God hasn't really resolved my problems. I still abuse cocaine and alcohol. God has not removed these desires from me.

P.C.:   God is working, but it is too slow for you.

Restin: It's too slow.

P.C.:   Tell me a little about what kind of work God is doing in you.

Restin: That is hard. Last year, I didn't care about anything. This year I care about me and my marriage. I would like to get better. However, I can only go so far and the problem keeps coming back. I continue to go on cocaine and alcohol binges.

P.C.:   Have you sought addiction treatment?

Restin: That's not what I want. I want God to heal me. He healed the Gerasene demoniac, and that is what I want from God.

P.C.:   What if your healing will take time and involves addiction treatment? What if it means looking at some of the things in your life that hinder God's work in you?

Restin: I don't want to have to go through all of that. That is too hard. I just want to be delivered by God.

P.C.:   Sounds like there are some things in your life that need attention even if God delivers you from addiction.

Restin: What do you mean?

P.C.:   I heard you say that you considered yourself the black sheep of the family and that you were possessed by the devil. These issues are psychological and religious. They will be around after deliverance.

Restin: I suppose, but it would be so much easier if God could just do it all.

P.C.:   I think there is a lot of hard work ahead of you in counseling.

In this second session, I was attempting to move toward his personal mythology and the related themes in it. In the last portion of the interview, I introduced two themes that made up part of his personal myth or self-convictions and self-beliefs. These convictions and beliefs were that he was worthless and possessed by evil. Later on in that session I did a genogram—a three-generational description of his family of birth or origin. Through it he was able to identify some of the themes that contributed to making up his personal myth. We explored these themes in this second session and two subsequent sessions and traced how they had influenced his life from the time he was about seven years of age. We explored how these themes were related to his destructive and negative behavior. We mapped how he was living out a negative drama made up of the theme that he believed he would never amount to anything.

After identifying and mapping his personal myth, we explored what his preferred story would be. He saw himself as addiction free and on better terms with himself, his wife, and God. We then shifted to setting goals for his counseling. The first goal we set was to seek God's guidance on whether he needed to go into addiction treatment or whether he could overcome addiction without it. He decided to organize a prayer service of caring others to seek God's guidance on the matter. At the prayer service there were prayers for guidance and for deliverance from addiction to drugs and alcohol. Three days following the prayer service, he decided to go into the hospital for a four-week drug treatment program. Following drug treatment he came back to pastoral counseling to work on his personal myth, which was blocking the work of God in his life and his preferred story. His preferred story was to continue to recover from addiction and to work on improving his relationships with his wife and God. We then moved into the re-authoring stage of counseling.

MOVING TOWARD RE-AUTHORING THE PERSONAL MYTH

From attending to Restin's existential situation in the initial stages of counseling, I noticed that two frameworks influenced how he interpreted his experience. The first framework was based on biblical stories and particular texts from the Bible that he had learned from growing up in the church. The second framework was a personal mythology that operated mostly outside his awareness. While he consciously attempted to live out his understanding of his faith, his personal mythology constantly undermined his efforts. His personal mythology was made up of internalized frustrating relationships from his past that became a norm for evaluating his life and his experience in the world. It would manifest itself whenever he made an attempt to make something out of his life. The norm constantly reminded him of his inadequacy as a person and of his worthlessness. It told him that he was trapped in life and that there was no escape for him. It was a losing script that made it difficult for him to accept success at doing anything. He was in complete bondage to his personal mythology and did not completely understand what was making his life so miserable. He felt hopeless and helpless, because his personal mythology seemed to be the strongest force in his life.

However, his personal mythology was not the only force at work in his life. There were the Bible stories at work in him. When he allowed himself to focus on the Bible stories in his life, he became very realistic in his self-appraisal and could clearly see some of the areas of his life that needed to be attended to in counseling. He felt both challenged and supported by stories from Scripture. Yet, when his personal mythology dominated his life, he immediately lost both hope and his realistic self-appraisal. He began to see himself as a helpless victim of others who could do very little to improve his lot in life, and as a pawn in the hands of angry people. All the hurt and all the pain that he felt being a victim in the world surfaced, and he began to be overwhelmed. He lost his sense of self-esteem and began a growth-frustrating attitude of self-pity. He began episodes of self-destructive and self-sabotaging activity that included periodic cocaine and alcohol abuse. He felt like the world owed him something because of his abuse, and he wanted the world to give him reparations for his emotional wounds. Often his wife became the person he expected to pick up the pieces of his life, making things better. In short, Restin lost all confidence in himself and in the world around him. As a result, he retreated from himself and from the world in substance abuse.

It was obvious that Scripture played a growth-facilitating role in his life, while his personal mythology made him feel vulnerable and unable to cope. The latter left him with feelings of being overwhelmed, helpless, and unable to survive. When he was grounded firmly in Scripture, however, he felt related to himself, others, and God, and that he was moving toward wholeness. At those times he felt emotionally and spiritually integrated as a person, and he had a more positive outlook on life. He identified with Bible stories that had eschatological plots of finding hope in the midst of tragedy. When his life was linked with God's Story through individual Bible stories, he felt his life had direction and purpose.

From the initial "intake" interviews with both Restin and his wife, it became obvious to me that he and his wife felt that Scripture and church should play a greater role in his life. Scriptural "glasses" enabled him to visualize himself and the world in far different ways from those of his "victim glasses." Thus, the goal in counseling became to increase the positive role of Scripture in his life and to lessen the role of victim analysis.

From the vantage point of role-taking theory, Restin alternated between the two positions in giving perspective to his experience. This alternation is very common and expected.[1] It appears that role-taking is motivated by a crisis that propels a person to identify with Bible stories and characters that are similar to the person's situation. The result is that the situation of the person in crisis is structured in the light of Scripture, and certain predictable patterns can be expected based on the story in Scripture. However, this patterning and structuring of experience is temporary. The person eventually returns to the everyday characteristic way of patterning experience.

Restin was facing a crisis in his life. Consequently, he turned to Bible stories and characters to gain some resolution and perspective on his problem. He allowed Bible stories and characters that were familiar to him to temporarily structure his life. When this happened his life took on added meaning. However, the everyday, mundane way of viewing his life would return to the center stage and assert its power. This everyday, mundane perspective is what made up his personal mythology. It could not be easily replaced. His personal mythology had to be addressed in pastoral counseling before it could be modified.

Below, close attention is paid to the actual biblical stories and other passages that Restin felt were central to his pilgrimage in life. Once these particular biblical passages are identified, a literary analysis of the stories and texts is employed, revealing Bible images, metaphors, and themes that were at work in shaping Restin's life.

Jesus Heals the Gerasene Demoniac

Then they arrived at the country of the Gerasenes, which is opposite Galilee. As he stepped out on land, a man of the city who had demons met him. For a long time he had worn no clothes, and he did not live in a house but in the tombs. When he saw Jesus, he fell down before him and shouted at the top of his voice, "What have you to do with me, Jesus, Son of the Most

High God? I beg you, do not torment me"—for Jesus had commanded the unclean spirit to come out of the man. (For many times it had seized him; he was kept under guard and bound with chains and shackles, but he would break the bonds and be driven by the demon into the wilds.) Jesus then asked him, "What is your name?" He said, "Legion"; for many demons had entered him. They begged him not to order them to go back into the abyss.

Now there on the hillside a large herd of swine was feeding; and the demons begged Jesus to let them enter these. So he gave them permission. Then the demons came out of the man and entered the swine, and the herd rushed down the steep bank into the lake and was drowned.

When the swineherds saw what had happened, they ran off and told it in the city and in the country. Then people came out to see what had happened, and when they came to Jesus, they found the man from whom the demons had gone sitting at the feet of Jesus, clothed and in his right mind. And they were afraid. Those who had seen it told them how the one who had been possessed by demons had been healed. Then all the people of the surrounding country of the Gerasenes asked Jesus to leave them; for they were seized with great fear. So he got into the boat and returned. The man from whom the demons had gone begged that he might be with him; but Jesus sent him away, saying, "Return to your home, and declare how much God has done for you." So he went away, proclaiming throughout the city how much Jesus had done for him. (Luke 8:26-39)

In this section, narrative criticism is used to explore the function of the story of the Gerasene demoniac. The aim is to understand better how its literary and spiritual power attracted Restin. The methods at work here are the exploration of the drawing power of Bible stories, and examining similarity and identification.

Because Restin thought of himself as possessed by Satan, he had a particular interest in exorcism, so the story of the Gerasene demoniac attracted his attention. Let us explore the rhetorical power of this Bible story.

In Robert C. Tannehill's narrative examination of the

Gerasene demoniac, he focuses on the function of the narrator in the story.[2] For him the narrator is the literary instrument used for getting the story told.[3] The instrument is a character in the story who has an actual role. The narrator usually articulates the important values and beliefs to be affirmed by showing these values and beliefs to those addressed.

Luke 8:26-39 presents the Gerasene in one of the leading healing stories. Tannehill highlights how the book's narrator presents the interaction between Jesus and the one who is possessed. The narrator first brings the presenting human need into focus.[4] Tannehill points out that the "narrator controls the readers' experience in part through deciding what needs and tasks will be the center of attention in the story."[5] Through the use of the narrator in the healing stories, the reader or hearer will react to events in light of how the afflicted person's needs are presented. According to Tannehill, such a narrator tends to enable the reader or hearer to identify with the needs of the afflicted. The narrator can increase or lessen the identification either by expanding the scene in intricate detail or by making summary statements. Tannehill points out that the narrator in Luke has a flair for pathos. That is, the narrator increases the reader or hearer's sympathy for the afflicted by using certain touches that increase identification.[6] In the case of the Gerasene demoniac, the emphasis is on the wild behavior of the man involved.[7] Because the narrator highlights the needs of the afflicted, this also highlights the importance of Jesus' response to those in need. It is Jesus who responds to and meets the needs of the afflicted in the healing story. It is in his response to the afflicted that we see the overarching purpose of God's salvation drama as it is disclosed in Luke's narrative writing. The purpose is to portray Jesus as fulfilling God's salvation drama to set at liberty those who are captive.[8]

For Tannehill, the clue to understanding this text is the role of the narrator. The importance of the narrator is that it is the vehicle the text creates so that the particular story can transcend its original social and historical context.[9] It is through the narrator that the continuing message of salvation can have its impact on the present. The narrator has the capacity to draw the reader and listener into the story so that they can become part of God's salvation drama. Through the narrator, the original purpose of the text can be transmitted to the present. Since the narrator enables the dynamics of the story to transcend space and time in ways the author may not have intended, it is important to explore how a present-day counselee and pastoral counselor might be influenced by biblical stories. The key to such an exploration is what Tannehill calls pathos. As already indicated, pathos refers to pain associated with life and how this is dramatized by certain afflicted characters in the text. Restin saw a similarity between the story of the Gerasene demoniac and his own cocaine addiction. In particular, Restin saw his problem as more than a psychological problem or an addiction to a substance; he saw it as a battle and a struggle against satanic powers. He firmly believed that he was in the clutches of an evil power that he could not overcome by himself. He believed that he needed divine help and the help of many caring and praying others to obtain liberation from a bondage to Satan.

It was Restin's identification with the pathetic character who was possessed that made the story important for Restin. In fact, it is precisely the intent of the narrator that such an identification take place. Consequently, it was Restin's belief that he too could obtain his release from bondage through an act of God.

As a pastoral counselor, I had to take seriously Restin's description of his plight and circumstances. I had to learn to see and experience the world as he saw and experienced the world. Consequently, I discovered that one of the basic tools for learning to be empathetic with Restin was the story of the Gerasene demoniac itself. That is, to understand Restin, I had to learn to allow this particular biblical story to shape my own way of looking at the world. My own realization was that the more I allowed this story to speak to me and shape me, the more empathetic I would be toward Restin, and the better my diagnostic assessment of Restin would be.

Employing the method of attending to the drawing power of this story, the method of exploring similarity, and the method of identification made me more understanding of Restin's needs. One of the things these methods did was to help me take seriously Restin's belief that he was trapped in what he experienced as satanic bondage. He believed that there was a power outside his human will that was so powerful it required divine intervention. The belief that Restin had of being possessed by a satanic force outside oneself is considered "precritical." In Paul Ricoeur's mind, critical thought refers to separating what is truly historical from what is pseudo-historical.[10] Critical thinking rejects the notion that there is a three-tier universe of a heaven, earth, and hell. The idea that there is a force in life independent of historical reality which intervenes in reality is considered unhistorical and precritical thinking.

If I had felt that Restin's thinking was entirely precritical, my goal would have been to move Restin away from this precritical thinking, because it was magical and antithetical to the therapeutic process. There was undoubtedly a magical and triumphalistic quality to his expectation. However, my own assumptions about the forces of evil in life and the role of Scripture in the lives of persons who have become its victims would not allow me to dismiss his beliefs in a cavalier way. Restin experienced drug addiction as a mysterious form of possession over which he had very little control. It was obvious his addiction had a destructive and evil hold on him. I too believed that there was a power in Bible stories that confronted this evil he faced.

Restin took the story of the possession of the Gerasene demoniac as literally true. He never questioned its validity. Rather, he believed that God could do the same thing today. However, he believed that God would not exorcise spirits in him or show him compassion, because he possessed a deep tragic flaw or personal defect. He believed that no one could love him, and this included God. He believed he had a personal defect that prevented God from showing compassion on him.

Role-taking theory also assists with employing the methods of identification and similarity. Role-taking theory helps explain why he took the Gerasene demoniac story literally. From his childhood, Restin had had a long history of role-taking with Bible stories. He was now facing a crisis; therefore, he sought to resolve it by relying on Scripture. Consequently, he identified with the pathetic character and began to see the world through the eyes of the Gerasene demoniac. Role-taking theory indicates that people not only identify with the role of human characters; they also simultaneously take on the role of God in a story. That is, one anticipates that God will act in the situation one confronts as God acted in the life of the figure with whom one has identified when that figure was confronted with similar circumstances.[11]

Restin was able to make the human role identification. However, because of his perceived tragic personal flaw, he was not able to envisage the same outcome for himself as the Gerasene had experienced. His personal mythology prevented the full task of human role-taking with God's role.

There was a real danger that Restin actually expected to overcome addiction without having to do very much himself. At this point, triumphalism surfaced as an additional theme in his personal mythology. Triumphalism is a belief that one can be freed from suffering by a magical act and that there is no personal effort needed. Restin understood very well that drug addiction had demonic power over him. He also knew that he could not overcome it alone. His problem was that he needed to make the effort to assume more responsibility for those areas of his life where he did have some control. For example, praying for release from the power of Satan was not enough by itself; he also needed to enter into drug treatment. He needed to expand his world view to include a view of exorcism as a process. That is, in most cases, the sudden end of addiction does not come immediately following prayer. Rather, prayer, drug treatment in a drug treatment program, and follow-up in a 12-step program are all dimensions of deliverance from drug addiction. In other words, a holistic approach, including prayer for deliverance and adopting a process view of deliverance, was the root to healing for Restin.

Restin's role-taking was helpful because it enabled him to identify with a narrative where the plot held out hope for him. He desperately wanted to believe that he too could experience the deliverance of the Gerasene demoniac.

Because of my own beliefs about the transforming power of Bible stories, I accepted Restin's belief that this story could have some transforming effect on him. I saw the story as a force that might overthrow his personal mythology.

THE METHOD OF EXPECTATION AND CHALLENGE

The purpose of re-authoring is to use reason to gain distance from the personal mythology in order to discern the possible alternatives that could lead to a preferred story. What this meant for my work with Restin was to help him identify the themes of his personal mythology and to discuss them in therapy. My role was also to help him discern how his belief in the story of the Gerasene demoniac could be acting to dethrone his personal mythology and to lead him to a healthier mythology. This method of bringing the Bible story into dialogue with the personal mythology is called expectation and challenge. My goal was to help him stop alternating between his everyday, mundane personal mythology and the Bible story. The hope was that he could revise his personal mythology through more consistent role-taking with Scripture.

Restin was aware of certain themes in his personal mythology when he came to counseling. These themes included feelings of being possessed by the devil, God's slowness to love him, conviction of his unlovability, being a black sheep and bed-wetter, and being a disappointment to others. However, he was not aware of his triumphalistic expectations. He had above-average intellectual abilities and often used them to rationalize the reasons why he could not act on his insights. Consequently, insight was not an effective motivating force in his life.

Restin was not aware of how his identification with Bible stories was at work in his life. He realized that he was interested in Bible stories, but he was utterly unaware of their potential for healing his personal mythology. He needed to learn more about how to allow these stories to take their healing initiative in his life. My role became to help him reflect on the dialogue between his personal mythology and the Bible stories that was occurring within the depths of his being.

Much in the early stages of counseling related to how he could alter his view of his worthlessness in light of the story of the Gerasene demoniac. He indicated that there was only one way for him to do this; namely, actually experiencing the same deliverance or exorcism the possessed man in the Bible story had experienced. Restin desired to be embraced by human and divine role-taking. My response was to help him discern the subtle and hidden exorcisms already taking place in his life as a result of the Bible story. I had to help him look beyond his impatience and desire for immediate healing, to envision new possibilities that the story was already offering him.

This expectation of receiving immediate healing from drug addiction was a manifestation of the triumphalism that was part of his personal mythology. He believed that God would do things for some people even when they did not cooperate with God. He felt that God was slow in responding to his need only because of his unworthiness.

The struggle between the Bible story and his personal mythology took the form of an important life decision. The question was whether he would enter drug treatment, or attend a healing service for exorcism without going to drug treatment.

45

At this point in the re-authoring, I raised an additional question for him to consider. I asked whether he could do both. My goal was to get him to reflect on the tension between the expectation of sudden healing and the process of healing. Eventually, he did decide on both options: He went to drug treatment, but a healing service was performed by his pastor prior to his commitment to enter into treatment.

As Restin's reflection proceeded in counseling, he finally decided to embrace both avenues that were open to him—scriptural healing and modern drug treatment. His acceptance of modern treatment was an altering of his personal mythology to incorporate treatment into the story of the Gerasene. That is, he began to envisage himself as a full participant in his own healing along with the help of others and the help of God. He began to visualize himself as a person who could make a difference in his own life. He was no longer expecting God and others to do things for him without his involvement. His expectation that God would immediately make a difference in his predicament had been triumphalistic, and thus his willingness to cooperate meant that he was beginning to alter these triumphalistic expectations. A significant dimension of his personal mythology was beginning to change. He was moving closer to full participation in scriptural role-taking.

Prior to his decision to enter drug treatment, another theme of his personal mythology emerged. This was the theme of entitlement. His entitlement was related to the theme of triumphalism in that he felt he deserved to receive healing from his early childhood wounds without having to make any effort himself. Entitlement is deeply rooted in the frustration of primary narcissistic needs for mirroring responses by significant others, and it is manifested in the belief that one is entitled to live one's life strictly on one's own terms.[12]

Restin interpreted the theology of grace through his feelings of entitlement. Although he felt God was slow to love him because of some personal defect, he also believed that he was entitled to God's grace, and he took the theology of justification by grace very seriously. He believed in the unmerited favor of God. In the re-authoring process we focused on grace as a free gift and a transforming power that required faith. The question we pondered in counseling was whether or not grace required personal faith to transform his personal mythology. Faith referred to his active cooperation with the grace that was at work in his life. The biblical phrase "grace through faith" became central to the therapeutic session. Eventually, Restin decided that grace needed his help, so he entered into a drug treatment program full-time.

When Restin made up his mind that grace required his active participation, he was altering his personal mythology and re-authoring it. He was gradually giving up the feelings of entitlement that he had developed as a result of internalizing negative relationships from the past. In other words, in order to alter his personal mythology, he was externalizing that which had been internalized early in his life. In the words of John Bradshaw, he was externalizing the toxic shame that was the root of his personal mythology.[13] Poor and frustrating relationships from his past had become an abiding source of frustration and left him with feelings of not being loved and of being unlovable.[14] He saw himself as defective as a result, and had deep feelings of personal embarrassment.[15] To externalize this shame, Restin had to engage in a therapeutic process where he felt some of his needs for acceptance and mirroring were being met. When he felt accepted, he could risk exposing his shame in the re-authoring process.

By way of summary, the story of the Gerasene demoniac hooked Restin through its drawing power and the narrator's use of pathos. Moreover, Restin's habit of biblical role-taking also assisted in the hooking. He allowed himself to be drawn into the story, and this identification led him to raise questions about his personal mythology in the setting of pastoral counseling. With the help of a pastoral counselor, he was able to reflect on ways to re-author his personal mythology in growth-facilitating ways.

THE JONAH COMPLEX

Restin had made significant progress in his treatment for addiction. He had entered drug treatment, and he had been successful in staying away from cocaine for about six months. He no longer had doubts about God's real care for him. He could actually see God at work in his recovery. He had invited God to be part of his treatment, and he was following the lead that God was giving him. He was now in a position where he could be responsive to the needs of others.

Restin had grown. He no longer believed he was as helpless as the Gerasene demoniac. Rather, he had matured to the point where he was re-authoring his personal mythology in significant ways. One incident led him to alter his personal mythology further.

Restin had found steady work after drug treatment. He worked in a warehouse keeping inventory and making sure that deliveries were ready when truck drivers came to pick up their deliveries. He was doing a good job and many people noticed how well he worked. Others also noticed that he seemed fairly mature and carried himself in ways they admired. They had no idea that he was recovering from cocaine addiction.

One day the boss's nineteen-year-old son began to ask him about the Bible. Restin did not know why the young adult came to him, for he had said nothing to him about being a Christian. No one at work knew of Restin's background or of his interest in religion or evangelism. Nonetheless, this young man came to him asking him religious questions.

At this point in the story it is important to note that Restin was black and the boss's son white. As Restin was finding success in recovery, the old theme of entitlement began to re-emerge in his life and dominate his thinking. Restin felt anger when he began to think this young adult wanted something from him. He began to say, "Why should I help him? He is the enemy. He is the reason why I have a drug problem. His kind has made it difficult for me. Why should I help him? He wouldn't help me." Restin again began to feel that he was entitled to live his life on his own terms without having to reach out to others.

When Restin told me about his attitude, I mentioned that God might have sent this young man to him to complete his healing. I mentioned that part of the 12-step program for overcoming addiction involved reaching out to others who have problems similar to one's own.[16] I interpreted his behavior as resistance to God's healing work taking place at the core of his being. He responded to my interpretation with the words: "It is as if I am Jonah." He went on to explain the meaning the story held for him and how it applied to him. He indicated that he didn't want God's love and mercy to extend to those he called the enemy and that he could feel what Jonah must have felt.

I wanted to suggest to Restin that God was drawing him into the story of Jonah for a reason. I began to look more closely at this story in order to discern how it was working to help him continue to re-author his personal mythology. Jonah, of course, was swallowed by a great fish after he boarded a ship to get away from God's call directing him to Nineveh.

Restin's habit of Bible role-taking was at work in his identification with the life of Jonah. Because the role-taking was accompanied by the expectation that he might be treated similarly to the character identified with, Restin began to explore the implications of the story for his life.

The Jonah Syndrome

Significant for understanding the importance of this story's approach is the role of the narrator. In telling the story, the narrator articulates the values and beliefs that are central to the story. In the Jonah story, the role of the narrator is to influence the listener or reader in a certain way. This role has been pointed out by James Limburg. He says:

> As the story winds down, the questions addressed to Jonah more and more become questions addressed to those listening to the story. Jonah, it becomes clear, is me! Thus, the story asks its hearers: Do you recognize yourself in the figure of Jonah? Do you detect in yourself symptoms of the Jonah Syndrome?[17]

The way in which the story is told actually draws the reader to identify with the character of Jonah. The telling of the story also leads the hearer to self-evaluation. The way the story was told to the original audience influenced them in certain ways, and a similar effect results when the person of today hears the story.

Because the basic methodology employed in the book of Jonah allows the narrator to influence the hearer, pushing the hearer to examine himself, much can be learned about Restin by making a narrative analysis of the Jonah story.

Prior to exploring the way in which Restin appropriated the Jonah story in re-authoring his personal mythology, it is important to note what some narrative critics have said about the Jonah syndrome. Some combine an analysis of the original audience with hypotheses about the way in which the storyteller addressed the specific needs of the original audience. Limburg sees the original audience as religious insiders whose attitude toward outsiders needed to be changed.[18] Other narrative critics place the Jonah story in the prophetic narrative genre, making its chief aim didactic.[19] This perspective says that the goal of the structure and form of the story is to persuade the original hearers to decide to live differently from the way Jonah lived. Ultimately, this view says that the message of the story is to warn the hearers or readers against narrow particularism.

My own view of the book of Jonah as narrative is that it is a story of the disclosure of reasons behind Jonah's refusal to embrace his vocational call. The early part of the story introduces God's call of Jonah and Jonah's negative response to that call. The next phase of the story is the account of the confrontation between God and Jonah regarding Jonah's negative response. The third phase of the story is Jonah's reluctant decision to do what God had asked him to do. Finally, in chapter 4, verse 2, Jonah begins to reveal to God why he refused to be obedient to God initially, telling God that he knew God to be gracious, merciful, slow to anger, and abounding in steadfast love. Here Jonah is saying he resented God showing love to those who were the enemies of Israel. Even though God had loved him and the Israelite people, he wanted to dictate to God how this love could be shared with others.

Clearly, Jonah was a person who had known God's love. However, he was reluctant to allow God to share this love with others he deemed outsiders. The message of the book is addressed to those whose attitudes were similar to Jonah's. Moreover, those who were drawn into the story, it would be hoped, would eventually come to the same conclusion. That is, they would examine their own attitudes toward God sharing God's love with those who were considered outsiders or enemies. One could expect that the story of Jonah would have a similar impact on the hearer of today. But for Restin?

Restin had begun to work through some of his real difficulties with drug addiction. He had discovered that God had not abandoned him as he had previously thought, and indeed that God was very much at work in his life. Restin had found a job that he liked and was doing very well with it.

As recounted earlier, during Restin's recovery the boss's son began to approach him seeking some advice and counsel. This young man needed guidance in areas with which Restin was very familiar. Restin began to realize that God had led this young man to him. I also believe that this was an opportunity for Restin to complete his recovery by reaching out to others like himself. However, Restin initially resented God's sending this young man to him. He was angry at God, and refused to reach out to the young man.

In the counseling relationship, I raised with him a question about whether he really wanted to be healed completely. I explored with him the point that perhaps his refusal to reach out was a form of resistance to becoming a whole person. He responded to me by reasserting that this young man was white. He insisted he would not have had the problems with addiction in the first place had it not been for racism. He protested with the words: "Why should I reach out to help the enemy when they wouldn't help us?" In so doing, Restin was making the boss's (white) son symbolically responsible for his ills (in this case addiction)—an example of external locus of control, or making someone else responsible for one's own problems. He had obviously lost ground in his growth, because he returned to an earlier theme of his personal mythology. The pattern of alternation was still at work.

As Restin talked, he began to return to Jonah. He became more aware how his attitude was similar to Jonah's. He grew quiet as he reflected on the implications of the Jonah story for his own life and also commented on the plant on which Jonah had taken pity and how God had used the plant to convey a message to Jonah. He then acknowledged that he had a Jonah complex.

For the next few months, the Jonah story provided the basis for our counseling together. The main focus of the counseling was on whether God had his and Jonah's best interests at heart.

The story of Jonah provided insight into Jonah's anger and resentment toward God and God's nature. The story raised the issue of Restin's vocation—the need for meaningful work. Yet, there was something in Restin that prevented him from responding positively to God's call. However, the story did force him to become self-reflective and to advance the externalization process. He began to discern that he had to embrace his vocational call if he was to continue to re-author his personal mythology. Taking this next step in the re-authoring process was very difficult for him. The personal mythology held on and resisted letting go. At the end of our counseling relationship, he had achieved significant growth. However, there was no triumphal victory. His was a lifelong task of revising and re-authoring his personal mythology following the lead of Bible stories.

Restin identified with the story of Jonah and the story of the Gerasene demoniac. Before Restin realized it, these two episodes had pulled him into a much larger Story; he began to see himself as part of God's salvation drama. He was being led toward vocation. In other words, the externalization process had brought to his awareness that he was beginning to take on a completely different personal mythology. He had grown considerably and had done significant work altering his personal mythology. There was less alternating between old personal mythology and the new emerging personal mythology.

We return to Restin again in chapter 4. At that point the discussion shifts from personal mythology to marital mythology. Restin and his wife, Sue, are used to illustrate the transformation of marital mythology. The discussion of the influence of violence begun here continues in chapter 3.

CHAPTER THREE

PERSONAL MYTHOLOGY
AND ABUSE

In this chapter the role of violence in the formation of personal mythology is examined. Second, the role of Scripture in maintaining a positive mythology in a rape victim's life is explored.

What follows is the story of a counselee who found a particular psalm very helpful in her recovery from a brutal rape and attempt on her life. This story was written by the rape victim after several months of pastoral counseling with me.

JOAN'S STORY

On my way to work Wednesday, May 13, 1992, I listened to a radio minister preach about sexual sins in the congregation. When I left work on my way to Bible study, the same minister was preaching the same sermon. This was the first time I had been able to attend a Bible study at my church this year. At Bible study, I was moved by the lesson, which was about Lot's offering his two daughters to a mob of male homosexuals who wanted to have sexual relations with Lot's guests. Later, Lot's daughters engaged in incest with their father. I now believe that the sermon and Bible study were preparing me for what happened to me that night.

I left church and headed for home. About midway, I heard a huge explosion at the rear, passenger-side window of my car. Before I could turn around to see what the loud noise was, a man had broken into my car and put a gun to my neck. He told me he just wanted my pocketbook. But he told me to drive straight ahead and warned me that if I made the wrong move, he would blow me away. I realized my life was in great danger.

As I was directed to drive through a low-income housing project, the man pressed the gun to my neck and threatened over and over to kill me. His voice was extremely nervous; I could not see him. He directed me to a dark street and the driveway of a boarded-up abandoned house. After I stopped the car, the man pulled me out of the car and made me spread my hands over the top of the car. He pulled my skirt up and realized I had on pants. Then he made me take off my clothes. As he attempted to rape me from behind, I began praying out loud. He told me to shut up or he would kill me. He was unable to rape me from behind. Giving up, he pushed me around to the front of the car (still behind me) and put a scarf over my eyes.

There was a long delay and rustling before he spoke again. Then he told me to get on top of the hood of my car. I did what he said. He climbed on top of me and raped me. When he had finished, he pulled me down off the car and told me he was going to take me home. By that time, I was trembling all over. He raised up the car trunk, shoved me in it, and shut the lid.

As the man backed the car out of the driveway, I began to pray to God for mercy. Slowly, I moved my hand over the front side of the trunk, looking for a way out. I found a small button, about the size of a quarter, pressed it in, and released the trunk. I peeked out of the trunk but was afraid I would severely injure myself if I tried to get out while the car was moving at high speed. So I reluctantly allowed the lid of the trunk to click back in place.

I began to pray to God for mercy again. The man drove me around for what seemed to be a very long time. I continued to pray and ask God for mercy. And finally, the man started stopping and going. I remembered the button and tried to find it again. I found it, peeped out, and saw a familiar white church that appeared to glow like white neon lights and its denominational symbol like neon red. I knew where I was.

In a few minutes, he stopped the car in front of a car wash where three people were standing out on the sidewalk. I jumped out of the trunk and wrapped a jacket around my waist. I ran frantically to the two cars right behind my car. But the people drove around me. Then I ran across the street to the car wash where a man was washing his beautiful royal-blue truck. The truck was high up from the ground. I ran up to him and told him I had been raped and was afraid that the man was going to come back and get me. I asked him if I could get in his truck. He said, "No, get away from me." I begged him, but he told me to go away.

I saw a man running and within a few minutes, he drove his car in front of the blue truck and threw the passenger door open. I ran to the car, but before I could sit down, I saw another man flagging down the police. The police officer began asking me questions. He gave me his yellow rain pants and jacket to put on.

Outside the police car was a young woman who was peeping in the window. I asked the police officer if she could get in the car with me. He hesitated, but agreed. When the woman got in, I started crying. She held me and petted me, telling me it was going to be all right. She said she had been raped before, but didn't tell anyone because no one would believe her. Then she told me that she was addicted to drugs. I asked her what kind. She said, "crack cocaine." I asked her if she wanted to be delivered. She said, "Yes." I raised up from her lap, held her hands, and we prayed a prayer for deliverance from addiction.

When the police were ready to take me back to the scene of the crime, the young woman and the two men who helped me (probably cocaine addicts) came to say goodbye. I hugged them and thanked them. The police took me back to the scene of the crime, to the police station, and to the hospital. They released me from the hospital at 5:30 A.M. on Thursday.

On Thursday, one of my friends read Psalm 116 to me. I was astounded because Psalm 116 recounts exactly what happened to me.

> I love the LORD, because he has heard
>   my voice and my supplications.
> Because he inclined his ear to me,
>   therefore I will call on him as long as I live.
> The snares of death encompassed me;
>   the pangs of Sheol laid hold on me;
>   I suffered distress and anguish.
> Then I called on the name of the LORD:
>   "O LORD, I pray, save my life!"
>
> Gracious is the LORD, and righteous;
>   our God is merciful.
> The LORD protects the simple;
>   when I was brought low, he saved me.
> Return, O my soul, to your rest,
>   for the LORD has dealt bountifully with you.
>
> For you have delivered my soul from death,
>   my eyes from tears,
>   my feet from stumbling.
> I walk before the LORD
>   in the land of the living.
> I kept my faith, even when I said,
>   "I am greatly afflicted";
> I said in my consternation,
>   "Everyone is a liar."
>
> What shall I return to the LORD
>   for all his bounty to me?
> I will lift up the cup of salvation
>   and call on the name of the LORD,

> I will pay my vows to the LORD
> > in the presence of all his people.
> Precious in the sight of the LORD
> > is the death of his faithful ones.
>
> O LORD, I am your servant;
> > I am your servant, the child of your serving girl.
> > You have loosed my bonds.
> I will offer to you a thanksgiving sacrifice
> > and call on the name of the LORD.
> I will pay my vows to the LORD
> > in the presence of all his people,
> in the courts of the house of the LORD,
> > in your midst, O Jerusalem.
> Praise the LORD!

This was my story. I knew the Lord loved me before this incident. But the experience awakened a greater knowledge of God's faithfulness. Just as the psalmist did, I prayed out loud for mercy (vv. 1-2). I don't remember all the words that I said. I prayed as the fumes of carbon monoxide got thicker. I heard the gas splash back and forth as more fumes replaced the oxygen in the trunk. I felt I would soon be overcome by asphyxiation and die (v. 3). I cried out to God to save me from death (v. 4).

Every time I reflect on what happened to me, I am overwhelmed. God heard my prayer and answered so quickly. God heard my voice of supplication. God heard me when I cried out, "O God, save my life" (v. 4). I am convinced that God loves me, and I now have a greater love for God. As the Scripture states, "God is righteous, merciful and tenderhearted. God defended me, the simple, when I was brought to my knees" (vv. 5-6). I know God spared my life. Now, I've been saved twice.

Not only did God save me, but God allowed my soul to return to its resting place. "God snatched my soul from death" (vv. 7-8). God robbed the grave. And in a very short time (three weeks), God stopped my tears and removed the fear from my body, soul, and mind. And now, because "I can walk before God in the land of the living" (v. 9), I have faith, even when I say, "I am completely crushed and knocked out." I recognize that no one is more dependable than God (vv. 10-11). God is faithful.

"How shall I repay God for all he has done for me?" (v. 12) I now boldly and fervently answer with my promise: TO PRAISE GOD AS LONG AS I LIVE. "I will lift up the cup of salvation and call on the name of God." "I will pay my vows to God before all of his people" (vv. 13-14). I know that I am "precious in the eyes of God." I am God's servant and I will offer sacrifices of praise and call upon the name of God (vv. 15-17).

I could not wait to "pay my vows to God before all the people in the House of God" (vv. 18-19). I went to church on Sunday to pay my vows. For the first time in my life, I shouted in expression of the joy of my salvation. It was bursting uninhibitedly within me. I stood before the congregation and made my testimony about the awesomeness of God. I knew that there were rumors spreading fast, and I wanted the people of God to hear my report. I shared the detail of my distress and deliverance. And as long as I live, I will and must keep my vows to God to praise God for salvation, mercy, and goodness.

The miracles of this traumatic incident continue to unfold in my life. The miracle of the button was the best of all. When the police discovered my car, it had been completely burned. They told me he torched the car to destroy evidence. My car was taken to a salvage yard. The detective invited me to see it. I was amazed to see how badly the car was burned, everything except the trunk. Several people who owned Mercedes told me they did not have buttons in their cars, but I was convinced that I had one. When we opened the trunk and looked for the button, we did not find one. There was no opening in the trunk where the button could possibly be. But all things are possible with God. God worked the miracle of the button in my life. It was a supernatural button just for me. I experienced the Lord's compassion and power. The message of the miracle and God's compassion and power must be made known to all people. God does save. God does deliver. God saved my life and as long as I live, I will offer prayers of thanksgiving and praise to Our Mighty, Awesome God.

During one of my counseling sessions, Dr. Wimberly asked me if I felt like a victim or a survivor. I told him I felt like a survivor. But more and more as time passes, I feel like I'm more than a survivor. I am a conqueror. I am no longer in a spirit of bondage because of this incident. I have been liberated through the Spirit of Adoption by God. God has not given me the spirit of bondage, but the Spirit of Adoption (Romans 8:15).

Comments on the Case Study of Joan

As I listened to her, I watched her demeanor and observed her affect. This was about three days after the rape. I also monitored my own reaction to make sure my responses were helpful and appropriate to her experience. I was surprised that there was very little sign of depression in her face, posture, or voice. I recognized this as the initial stage of reaction to rape and that appropriate denial was at work to protect her from being overwhelmed by intense feelings. However, I thought that I would gently introduce my observation about the absence of dejection and depression. She smiled and said, "I am not depressed right now, because I am alive." She continued, "God answered my prayer."

I was dumbfounded by her response, and it showed on my face. I asked her, "How did God answer your prayer when you have been through such an ordeal?" She then responded, "I thought the man was going to kill me."

Joan then said that she had been relying on two Scriptures to help her since the horrible event. She said her feelings toward God could be summarized by Psalm 116. For her, God heard her supplication and delivered her from the hands of death. She had nothing but praise for God. Joan thought she was going to be killed. She said that when she felt vulnerable and was about to submit to the bondage of the event, she recited Romans 8:15, saying that God had not given her the spirit of bondage but the Spirit of adoption. Joan saw her rescue as the work of God, and she experienced God as a real presence despite the ordeal.

As the weeks passed, there were times when she had flash-backs and feelings of being unprotected—of being completely vulnerable. There were trying moments of many kinds. Yet, despite periods of depression, she continued to maintain her faith that God was present in her life in a very powerful way.

As part of her therapy, she went to visit the ruins of her car. She found some valuables that were not destroyed by the fire. She also searched for the button or trunk release that allowed her her freedom. However, there was no button. Several persons helped her to look for it. This confirmed in her mind that her deliverance was God's miracle.

Sometime after the rape, the feelings of depression and vulnerability surfaced to be explored in therapy. For about four weeks following the rape, Joan was very dependent on others. She felt she was burdened with unnecessary irritants that came as a result of the disruption of her life. For four weeks her friends were there for her and did what was needed. However, after the four-week period she felt that her friends were slowly withdrawing from her. She then began to realize that she needed to do the vital things that she had been postponing. She began to make sure that she went for follow-up medical tests for pregnancy and AIDS. She attended to the replacement of insurance information and vital identification that had been destroyed in the fire. As she accomplished these tasks, she slowly began to come out of her depression.

Joan also felt that she must not keep quiet about what had happened to her. She interpreted verse 14 of Psalm 116 to mean that she was to respond to God's deliverance from death by making sure that others heard what God had done for her. She wanted to "pay my vows to the Lord in the presence of all his people." Joan therefore shared her experience at her church and over the radio. She went on TV with her identity disguised and reported the rape so that others could be warned. She realized she was putting her life in danger, but she felt more at ease because of the disguise. As a result of her effort to make known what had happened to her, a suspect was identified and other women who had been raped by the same suspect came forward. It was this effort to tell it all and her effort to help those who were victims of violence that kept her from sinking into deep depression. Although Joan made a remarkable response to being raped, she did face some real emotional danger. To understand the risks she faced, let's explore some theories of abuse put forward by pastoral theologians.

SOME THEORIES ABOUT THE PSYCHOLOGICAL CONSEQUENCES OF ABUSE

The underlying assumption here is stated clearly by Christie Cozad Neuger. She says:

> The church, despite its embeddedness in patriarchy, has often been a place of healing, refuge, and empowerment for women. It has served as a place of leadership and community. The power of God's Spirit to empower, even in the midst of oppression, is a clear beacon of hope. The church and its representatives must work to dismantle patriarchy and to bring justice and wholeness to the women and men in its midst.[1]

Nancy Ramsay echoes a similar concern for the role of religion in empowering women.[2] She points to the image of God's compassion, vulnerability, and presence within the life of human beings as empowering for women. She talks about joining God's redemptive, transformative power that empowers women.[3] She is among those who have encountered the tradition within Scripture in a way that frees, despite its patriarchal language.

One of the principal assumptions undergirding my analysis is that Scripture contains within it a drawing, transformative power that has the ability to communicate to those who are oppressed and abused in ways that call them to wholeness. The power calls people to grow beyond the effects of oppression and abuse. This power is contained in many narratives of the faith and encourages persons to be courageous survivors. Most stories of the Bible do not involve people who have conformed to idolatrous and oppressive beliefs held about them. Rather, the stories seek to make relative, challenge, and dethrone destructive self-beliefs that hold people in bondage. It is the liberating power of the Bible story that some women discover who have been victimized by violence.

There are some Bible narratives that are not liberating or helpful for women or men. They seem to have tragic outcomes and plots. An example is the story of Tamar in 2 Samuel 13:1-29. Although Tamar, the daughter of David, was raped by her brother, King David would not discipline his son, since he was the first-born. However, there are many other stories that do offer liberating possibilities to women and have been used by them.

So there are resources in the biblical narrative for women who are victims of violence. However, it is important to talk about the negative effects of violence on women before delving too far into a discussion of the role of Scripture. Nancy Ramsay describes the consequences of sexual abuse on a survivor's spirituality and emotional life.[4] Of particular importance, she says, is the personal mythology that develops as the result of sexual abuse perpetrated by significant others early in the survivor's life. Crucial themes in the development of a negative personal mythology include (1) blaming oneself for what happened, (2) hiding the event and keeping it a secret, (3) maintaining the family myth of pseudo-happiness at all costs, (4) feeling at fault for all the family problems, (5) hiding true feelings, (6) holding in anger, and (7) trying to remain sensitive to the needs of others at the expense of self. Ramsay points out that the sexually abused survivor becomes emotionally anemic. That is, she has an inordinate need to control her feelings. Some learn to be victims and not survivors and begin to act out the feelings of worthlessness through promiscuous relationships and substance abuse. Many become alienated from their "bodied self" as well.

Shame can be another component of the anemic reaction. Ramsay calls shame an inner sense of being insufficient and diminished. It is the "self judging the self."[5] Incest and sexual abuse force shame inward and the self becomes defective. Repeated sexual abuse constitutes chronic trauma, and the internalized damage to one's self-esteem continues beyond the trauma in terms of self-hatred and feelings of worthlessness.[6] Shame, then, undermines the person's sense of self, the capacity for love and religious belief, and healthy spirituality. It also makes the person want to disown hated parts of the self. A wedge is driven between the person and God that often makes it difficult to trust God.[7]

In addition to shame, being sexually abused brings with it the feelings of complete vulnerability and inability to feel protected.[8] Neither the world nor the family is safe. One finds it hard to believe in Jesus' love or in the all-powerful (Father) God who keeps people safe. Some victims of abuse try to engage in attempts to redeem God's love for themselves, because they feel they have failed God.[9]

The faulty and dangerous personal mythology that develops as the result of being sexually abused and victimized by violence is confirmed by Ramsay and others. JoAnne M. Garma talks about a form of learned helplessness that often accompanies physical battering and abuse.[10] She points out that women remain in battered relationships because they have learned that they have no control over being abused. Once women decide they have no control, they are convinced that they can never have any influence over the battering. Because repeated attempts to extricate the self from battered relationships have failed, the battered spouse often loses motivation to avoid battering and becomes passive. She also feels she is responsible for the battering behavior. This sets off a cycle of self-hatred, loss of self-respect, doubts about one's capacity for decision making, and a search for external confirmation of her inadequacy from others including the abusive perpetrator. She tries to affirm family values at the expense of self. When the church values submission of women to the authority of men, this reinforces the negative personal mythology that becomes a tragic losing script in the woman's life.

The personal mythology of abused and battered women is, indeed, reinforced by the cultural and religious values of patriarchy. Neuger analyzes some very negative effects.[11] Patriarchal values cause a disproportionate amount of depression and produce a survival strategy that demands self-devaluation and idolizing femininity. This depression is deepened by extended abuse, economic inequality, role stereotyping, androcentric bias in language and imagery, and resulting low self-esteem.

In these ways, depression and negative cultural images of women influence the development of negative personal mythologies. Overcoming these negative personal mythologies is extremely important if women are going to actualize their true nature as creations of God. One of the momentous strategies for assisting women in actualizing their full humanity is to name their own experience by telling their own stories. Neuger outlines a strategy of naming, which is very similar to the externalization process discussed earlier here. She recommends (1) separation from negative messages for the woman through telling her own story, (2) validating women's experiences, (3) greater affirmation by women in counseling, (4) authorization for being strong and self-accountable, and (5) negotiation for testing out new behavior in group settings.[12]

This material offered by feminist pastoral counselors is important, because it helps males not to assume that their experience of violence is the same as women's experience. There are some similarities. Yet, for males, society seems to open more avenues of escape from the effects of violence. There are patri-archal sanctions for women to be passive in the face of male vio-lence. The self-defense laws seem to be made for men and not women.

THE ROLE OF SCRIPTURE

Joan was not immune to the effects of rape. Rape is a violent crime that intends to inflict humiliation and emotional and bodi-ly harm on its victims. There was no way that Joan could avoid the devastating feelings and degradation associated with being victimized by rape. The fact that she relied on Romans 8:15—"For you did not receive a spirit of slavery to fall back into fear, but you have received a spirit of adoption"—is an indication that she was continually vulnerable in the weeks following the rape. She was constantly at risk of developing negative themes about herself because of the rape. She was in danger of becoming an emotional anemic, concluding that she had no value.

The fact that Joan mentions the story of Lot and his daughters (Gen. 19:1-11) as preparation for what happened to her that terri-ble night caused me to wonder about whether she felt betrayed and victimized by God. The story of Lot's willingness to sacrifice his daughters to save a group of men from homosexual rape seems very misogynic. This story was very tragic and without any appar-ent redemptive end. I explored with her whether she felt that God had given her up to rape as Lot had done. However, her response was continually that she was saved by God.

Below is a portion of an interview, where I used the method of reintroducing a Bible story to which she had made reference in order to explore her feelings about God.

P.C.:   When you first came to see me, you mentioned you thought that the story of Lot and his daughters prepared you for what happened to you on the unfortunate night.

I am really concerned that you might feel that God betrayed you.

Joan: I am not sure what you mean!

P.C.: Lot was going to give up his daughters to save men. This often happens to women.

Joan: I really don't feel like God sacrificed me to rape. Rather, I feel like I was saved from death by God.

P.C.: Rape is horrible and you keep saying that God saved you from a far worse fate. I feel I must keep checking to make sure that you are not far more devastated than you appear to be.

Joan: I really appreciate your concern. But, my feeling is that God rescued me. It was a terrible experience that I underwent, but I really know it was God who saved me. The man threatened to kill me. He even set my car on fire thinking that I was in it. It definitely was God who saved me.

P.C.: As a man I must continue to check to be sure you are not trying to spare my feelings.

Joan: I sense that it is difficult and sometimes my story makes you feel uneasy. But, truly, I am doing fine. Sometimes I feel shaky and vulnerable, but I assure you I am slowly moving back to my old self.

Later, I raised the issue of how she understood what had happened to her in terms of biblical language. She believed that Satan was the culprit and not God. In fact, we explored several years of what she called attacks by Satan since she had given her life over to the leadership of God. She actually felt that Satan was punishing her for her decision to be faithful to God.

Though Joan was a victim of rape, she became a survivor. She did many things that feminists suggest, such as seeking out the care of close women friends, and she told her own story and named her experience. She also relied a great deal on Psalm 116, which she said expressed her real feelings and gave voice to her experience. This psalm buttressed her positive personal mythology; there was very little movement toward negative themes. She felt loved and worthwhile, and God in Psalm 116 affirmed her. This psalm supported her personal integrity and helped her to deal courageously with being raped.

Psalm 116 is not normally thought of as narrative, in that it is a prayer of praise rather than a story. However, Psalm 116 has narrative dimensions to it that helped it act as a story in the life of Joan. These dimensions are worth exploring.

The Narrative Function of Psalms

Claus Westermann talks about the reconciling power of Psalms.[13] Human beings are made in the image and likeness of God, and in the process of helping us recognize our identity, the psalms allow us to speak to God. The psalms allow us as God's creations to speak to God in joy or sorrow. Westermann points out that the psalms have survived for centuries and through translation into many languages and still speak a living word to us today.[14] He finds their appeal to be that they address the unchanging basic constituents of human existence.

The psalms are poems that have arisen from what has taken place between God and human beings. They emerge from a set of circumstances and a specific event. Because they are made of the stuff of human and divine encounter, they are an appealing mirror for life.

The psalms are also intricately linked to human community. Worship in ancient Israel was the center of all life and the heartbeat of communal living. Consequently, the psalms could not be separated from the recounting of narratives in the worship life of the community.[15] They were central to the recounting of the individual and collective experience with God. In this sense, the psalms had a narrative dimension.

Some of the psalms contain explicit narrative elements.[16] For example, an individual psalm of praise often contains a narrative or a recounting of an event of deliverance. This is the case for

Psalm 116. It is called an individual narrative psalm of praise by Westermann.[17] This means that there is a part of the psalm that recounts the individual's experience with God. In this psalm there is a narrative of distress in verses 3-4 and 10-11; in verses 4, 8-9, and 16 there is the narrative of deliverance; and verses 5-7 and 15 contain the narrative of praise.[18] Psalm 116 with its narrative structure has the same drawing power as Bible stories do. The psalm also draws people into it because it speaks directly to their needs.

This was the testimony of Joan. She said she did not at first relate the psalm to her life. However, one of her friends indicated that her experience sounded like the experience of the person who wrote Psalm 116. Joan read the psalm and said that it articulated exactly the experience she was having. From that moment on, she found the psalm a great comfort. In the actual counseling sessions, I explored with Joan how the psalm was functioning in her life. I wanted to find out whether the psalm did more than help her to name her experience and tell her story. I wanted to know if the psalm functioned like other narrative forms in either supporting or challenging her personal mythology. I wanted to know whether the psalm had any influence in preventing her from taking on the bondage of slavery expressed in Romans 8:15.

Method of Similarity and Identification in Joan's Life

By employing the methods of identification, similarity, and expectation, it was discovered that Joan had a long history of role-taking with regard to Scripture. She first learned to take the role of biblical characters in Sunday school. Through the testimonies she heard from others and her own practice of role-taking, she learned to put herself in the role of biblical characters. She also learned to expect that events in her life might have outcomes similar to those of Bible stories.

Through Psalm 116 she saw herself as the person in the psalm who had been rescued by God. At this point the psalm held out to her the role of human sufferer. Her experience matched the experience of the sufferer in the psalm. Moreover, the psalm also enabled her to identify with the role of God so that she came to expect to be ministered to as the sufferer in the psalm was. In fact, she actually entered into dialogue with God and God ministered to her wounds.

Because of Joan's role-taking ability with Scripture, she was able to use a language and symbol system that kept her from being in conflict with God. In fact, her history of role-taking had shaped her perception of reality consistently since childhood. This role-taking led her to identify with the positive and hopeful stories of the Bible. Consequently, she would choose to see herself in Psalm 116 rather than as one of Lot's daughters in Genesis 19:1-11. She saw evil in light of how the Bible had shaped her view of reality. In the Bible, evil is attributed to Satan. Goodness is attributed to God. This biblical view of Satan as evil and God as good shaped her view of what happened to her.

Since the Bible shaped her perception of the world through role-taking, she was able to experience God's participation in her life despite the rape. Her role-taking experience with Scripture also led her to interpret her deliverance from the trunk as a miracle. Because role-taking shaped the way she perceived and interpreted what happened to her, the question could be raised: Was her experience real and valid? In other words, does role-taking theory explain away what actually took place? Was there no real experience behind her interpretation and perception?

In light of my own faith orientation and my own role-taking history, I tend to use role-taking theory in conjunction with a narrative theological perspective. This means that I deliberately allow the Bible stories and characters to shape my perception of reality. Consequently, role-theory helps me to understand how the Bible works in our lives. Moreover, I am interested in how the Scriptures work to set us free from negative personal, marriage, and family mythologies and how this liberating activity can be blocked. My faith perspective leads me to proclaim that there is an objective reality behind the liberating work of Bible stories. Therefore, because we share a similar biblical world view, and though there is no way objectively to prove that God miraculously freed her from the trunk of her car, I accept Joan's explanation of what happened to her.

My views have been influenced by William James and Wayne Oates.[19] James was concerned with the functional and pragmatic results that religious experience had on people. Oates was concerned to be sure that the pastoral counselor take a phenomenological approach to human experience by seeing religious experience through the eyes of the one who reports it. Consequently, my intent with Joan was to see her experience of rape as she saw it. However, I went farther, to test whether or not the way she understood it contributed to her growth and development. This means that I applied the pragmatic and functional test of James and the phenomenological attitude of Oates to Joan's experience.

As a pastoral counselor, I must raise the issue of how Scripture worked in Joan's life. I even sent her to a psychiatrist to ascertain whether she was using religion in a way that was blocking her ability to come to grips with the rape. The psychiatrist observed that she had truly made a good recovery from the rape. As a result of her own comments, self-appraisal, use of Psalm 116, and the observations of the psychiatrist and myself, I concluded that Scripture had played an important role in her recovery. In addition, her support group of women and pastoral counseling were instrumental in helping her to use role-taking with Scripture in a positive way. Because she was able to adopt a role, Scripture was able to bring healing resources to her life.

Role-taking and the Retelling of the Story of Hagar

Despite the patriarchal nature of some Bible stories, such as that of Tamar in 2 Samuel 13:1-29, Joan embraced the liberating narrative tradition that validated who she was as a person.

Her role-taking history and the positive support that she received from the support group of women and from pastoral counseling were the leading reasons for this. Following the termination of pastoral counseling, Joan found further support for her choice of liberating Bible stories. By retelling the story of Hagar, Joan gave me additional insight into the progress of her recovery.

Joan retold the story of Hagar in Genesis 16 and 21 as the rape of Hagar, who was an Egyptian slavewoman. She saw Sarah, Abraham's wife, as a real participant in the patriarchal system that victimized Hagar. Joan retold how Sarah took Hagar to Abraham to conceive a child for the childless couple, focusing on the fact that Hagar had no real decision in this matter since Hagar was a slave. Once Hagar conceived, Sarah began to treat Hagar very harshly and eventually forced Hagar out into the wilderness to die. In the wilderness, Hagar found God, and she and her son were rescued. About Hagar's salvation from her predicament Joan said, "While in the wilderness of Beersheba, Hagar cried out to God for help. God heard her cry and opened her eyes so that she was able to nurture her son into maturity. God had mercy upon Hagar and her son."

Joan summarized this story as the validation by God of Hagar as a worthy human being. She saw her own story as parallel to Hagar's journey. She felt that she was also validated by God when she was cast into the wilderness by the rapist.

By retelling the story of Hagar, Joan was allowing role-taking with Scripture to contribute to the continuation of her recovery from rape, because she was able to envisage a similarity between her situation and Hagar's. She saw God treating her in ways comparable to God's treatment of Hagar, and thus was able to confirm her own feeling of validation by God. She affirmed that her particular experience with God's liberation was not unusual but the continuation of how God dealt with Hagar.

Joan's retelling of Hagar's story confirmed that role-taking with the liberating tradition of scriptural narratives had a significant influence in her recovery from rape. The Hagar tradition helped her continued recovery. For Joan the Hagar story stood as God's true concern for those who have been victimized by the patriarchal circumstance. This story became a natural means for her to reenforce what God had already done in her life.

THE RE-AUTHORING PROCESS

My role as a pastoral counselor with Joan was to work within the parameters of the re-authoring process. Since she never developed a negative personal myth, re-authoring really involved supporting the existing positive personal myth undergirding Joan's life. The pastoral counseling task was to assist the work that the various narrative stories and elements were doing in her. This process included the following: (1) naming her own experience and giving voice to it as a means of separating the self from it; (2) mapping the influence of the event of rape on her life and on her personal mythology; (3) validating the work of Psalms as it created positive outcomes within her; and (4) helping her actualize these new possibilities.

As has already been indicated, Joan completed the first stage. She had given voice to her experience, and Psalm 116 helped her to give expression to what she felt. She had experienced death and feared for her life, and God had rescued her. Consequently, she told a narrative of distress as well as a narrative of deliverance.

In the therapy, we also explored the potential influence of the rape on her personal mythology. She reported that her self-esteem had come hard and that she was not going to give it up easily. She said she liked herself. She said she had no doubt that there was nothing more she could have done to protect herself from the attack, and thus she was not to blame. She indicated she was doing God's work by going to prayer meeting and she was not going to allow someone else's evil to drag her down.

I used the method of exploring the drawing power of Scripture with Joan to call her attention to what the psalm was doing in her life. Following this lead, she pointed out that she had got out her fire-charred Bible she had retrieved from her burned car and had read verses 14 and 18. In reading these verses she felt the psalm urging her to tell her story to others, not only for her own healing, but for the healing of many women out there who had been sexually abused. She felt that the rape was only a temporary setback, that God had already been tending her wounds, and that her tended wounds were becoming a source for the healing of others. In fact she was discovering a new ministry that she would not have otherwise considered, with the many hurting women besides herself. Joan felt that the psalm was not only gently urging her toward healing, but also that it was supporting her existing positive and personal mythology. She said she was happy with her response to what had happened and felt particularly good about coming forward and giving public voice to her experience on television, as a result of which the criminal rapist was apprehended. She believed that the psalm had had a strong role to play.

Through Joan's responses to my questions about the role of Psalms, she began to articulate new options for her life. She began to consider setting up support groups for abused women. She began to recognize that her wounds could be used for the good of others. She felt that not all abused women would have the same kind of experience she had had with God, but she felt she needed to extend what she knew to others through support groups.

Joan's case helps all of us to realize that moving from being victimized by rape to becoming a survivor and a conqueror is a pilgrimage and a process. As a pilgrimage, the healing of her wounds came as God influenced her life through the psalm and the lives of caring others. As she traveled the long road to recovery, she encountered God and people along the way. She even encountered new Bible stories that helped to further the healing of her pain. As a process, the encounter with Scripture and caring others set in motion a healing that unfolded a little at a time. Eventually, she found that her wounds were healed, and she was ready to begin a new journey in life. To date, her healing is not completed, but with every day she moves closer to it.

CHAPTER FOUR

MARITAL MYTHOLOGY AND THE IDEAL MATE

Personal mythology has been the main focus of this book thus far. We have defined personal mythology and the belief a person has about himself or herself and the world that influences the way the person lives in the world. The personal myth can be healthy, facilitating personal growth and development. Or it can be unhealthy, leading a person toward negative growth and tragic living.

It follows that personal mythologies influence many areas of one's life. They certainly have an impact on how a person selects a partner for dating, courtship, and marriage. Personal myths figure large in the formation of the "ideal mate image" that forms the foundation on which a marital mythology is built.

This chapter explores how Bible stories influence marital mythologies. We return to the earlier case study of Restin, to see how he and his wife, Sue, developed a marital mythology based on their personal mythologies.

MARITAL MYTHOLOGY

Marital mythology encompasses beliefs that each spouse or potential spouse has about an ideal mate. This ideal mate becomes the norm by which each person evaluates potential spouses.[1] The ideal is internalized and remains an archetype or pattern which persists until a mate is found. If the personal mythology and the themes in it are healthy, the ideal mate image is modified to fit the prospective actual mate. If unhealthy, the prospective mate is manipulated to fit the ideal mate expectations.

The marital mythology is made up of the two personal mythologies of the prospective mates.[2] The process of merging the two involves testing the prospective mate against the archetypal ideal that one has internalized. When the two prospective mates meet, and there is an encounter between the real and the ideal, several things can happen. There may be a natural fit of the two ideal-mate images, and of course this bodes well for the beginning of the marital relationship. Or, there may be a real discrepancy between the ideal and the real, and each of the two must then begin to revise the ideal in light of the real. This leads to a marital mythology that is grounded in a realistic appraisal of the prospective mate. When this happens, the marital mythology becomes a realistic one that can nurture each spouse. The third possibility is when one or both spouses encounter the disparity between the ideal and the real, and one or both spouses use coercive and manipulative measures to solicit from each other conformity to the ideal. Such an alternative can lead to conflict for the pair.

Actually, the first and third possibilities have within them seeds of potential conflict and inability to develop a nurturing marital mythology. In the case of the good fit, the fit can either be functional or dysfunctional. Whether the fit is functional or dysfunctional depends on the health of the personal mythologies that each person brings to the relationship. Unhealthy personal mythologies lead to unhealthy marital mythologies. Conversely, healthy personal mythologies lead to the development of healthful marital myths. In the third possibility, conflict always exists because each spouse is trying to get the other to conform to his or her ideal mate image.

It is important to explore the relationship between a negative personal mythology and the ideal mate image. As indicated, the ideal mate image grows out of a variety of experiences with significant others. The beliefs and themes that form the personal mythology often emerge from the internalized aspects of the relationships with significant others. The crucial concern is the attempt of the person with an unhealthy personal mythology to find an ideal mate who will either conform to or repudiate that mythology. For example, a person with a conviction of worthlessness and unlovability will have an ideal mate who either can lift him or her from the pits of worthlessness or will confirm that worthlessness.

Significantly, the personal mythology and the image of the ideal mate operate outside the conscious awareness of people. An ashamed person does not deliberately set out to find someone who will confirm his or her feelings of low self-worth. What happens is that the unconscious ideal-mate images dominate. Often, when one mate finds someone who repudiates the personal mythology, the found partner is manipulated to conform to the negative personal mythology of the other spouse. This happens because the negative personal mythology remains active in the unconscious and cannot rest until it prevails.

Bagarozzi and Anderson provide some theoretical bases for explaining how the personal mythology and the marital mythology support each other in the unconscious. They talk about an unconscious collusion.[3] In cases where there are negative personal mythologies and the couple reaches a workable marital myth, collusion is often at work. The process ensures that each spouse is protected emotionally from anxiety. Often there is a mutual protective contract that couples conspire to act out, and this acting out includes enacting certain themes of one's own personal myth as well as selected themes from that of the other. This process remains outside the awareness of both spouses.

The particular expectations that partners have for the ideal mate include self-validation, bolstering low self-esteem, alleviating depression, and reducing anxiety.[4] Through marriage those who have colluded to protect each other emotionally expect these needs to be met by maintaining the protective contract. Thus, there is still some measure of dissatisfaction when the protective contract does not permit these needs to be met. While these couples have agreed to coexist through an unconscious contract, there is still the hope and expectation that the ideal spouse expectations will be fulfilled.

We can see examples of these dynamics in the case of Restin and Sue.

Case Study

Sue often came to counseling with Restin. Their original complaint or presenting problem had to do with their marital relationship. Restin's complaints about his marriage were lack of communication, unfilled emotional needs, and financial disagreements. Sue also complained of these three things, but she added infidelity, and complaints that Restin was domineering and suspicious. Restin said that he had come for counseling at that particular time because he felt his life was leading to destruction and death. He said that death seemed to be an open option. He said he needed to come to a better understanding of himself and explore what it meant to surrender to God. Restin did report several incidents of attempted suicide fifteen years earlier.

When describing their courtship, Sue indicated that Restin was more of a receiver than a giver, although their courtship went very smoothly. They courted about one year before they began living together for about a year and a half. They married three years after they met. He also reported that things went smoothly at first. Restin indicated that the first sign of trouble came because Sue brought to their relationship a child. He felt that Sue treated his step-daughter more like an adult than she treated him.

Restin had been married prior to meeting Sue. He said he had felt very unhappy and trapped because he felt obliged to marry his first wife, who was pregnant with his child. His parents pressured him to do the "right and responsible thing." He said this was the biggest mistake he had ever made, and he indicated that the marriage never got off the ground. This relationship ended in divorce, and Sue and Restin both agreed that his first marriage had affected their relationship negatively.

It will be recalled from chapter 1 that Restin was forty-nine at the time of first counseling. His father was deceased and his mother was still alive, and he had three older sisters and one younger sister. He had a younger brother and one brother was deceased. Both parents had been employed outside the home. His father dropped out of school in the fourth grade, and his mother finished grade school. His mother and father were both church-goers, and his mother taught the children to believe in God. Restin said his mother was headstrong and did things her own way, and his father often responded to this with extramarital affairs. As for himself, Restin felt like he was literally the black sheep of his family and that his family saw him as an embarrassment.

Sue was fifty-five at the time of the counseling. Her father was deceased, her mother was still alive, and she had an older brother and an older sister. She described her parents as easy-going. Her mother had always worked. Her father had been an alcoholic who had extended dry periods, but he always returned to alcohol. Sue indicated she had a good relationship with her father but said she resented her father's drinking and felt that it was a weakness that caused her to think negatively about him. Sue indicated that she would often have to take care of her father when he was drinking, and this included providing financial assistance when he was irresponsible. She felt responsible for both her parents and would make her own needs secondary.

My assessment of their marital relationship related to what

they brought to the marriage from their families of origin. I assessed Restin as a person who was acting out a family-of-origin drama through self-destructive behavior that included his cocaine and alcohol abuse. He was reenacting the role of an irresponsible child who continually disappointed significant others in his life. Sue, on the other hand, realized that she was a co-dependent and cooperated in Restin's addiction to drugs and alcohol by continually taking care of him and getting him out of trouble. She realized that she had to change her way of relating to Restin. However, Restin was not willing for her to stop taking care of him. He experienced her wish to change her care-taking role toward him as abandonment and desertion. He would continually engage in self-destructive behavior to test whether she was serious. Her final resolve was to retire from her job so that she would not have the income to get Restin out of trouble. It was at that point in their relationship that Restin began to work steadily and bring home a paycheck.

Throughout the counseling, a constant religious theme was the theme of the wilderness. Restin felt that he was stuck in the wilderness because God let him down. He said God had not made things easy for him and was punishing him. Sue did not express any resentment about being in the wilderness, but felt she should make the most of her life despite it. She found that the biblical figure of Martha in Luke 10:38-42 represented her story, because like Martha she had a tendency to be overly concerned with work details rather than her relationship with Jesus. With this brief initial assessment of their marital relationship, we can now examine their marital mythology in more depth.

Assessment of Marital Mythology

The case data revealed that Restin and Sue brought to the marital relationship personal mythologies that became part of their expectations for each other. Restin and Sue both expressed disappointment that their emotional needs were unfulfilled in their marital relationship. Their feelings of unfulfillment represented a fundamental shift in their marital mythology. Reviewing the initial establishment of their marital myth and its development over time is crucial.

Restin and Sue developed a marital mythology that began as an unconscious contract that matched their personal mythologies. This unconscious marital contract was an agreement between the two of them to collude together to preserve each other's role in the family of origin and its accompanying personal mythology. We have seen that Restin had a personal mythology built around the feelings of being flawed and of very little worth. Added to this self-belief was the pattern of reenacting the role of an unwanted and unloved child. Accompanying the role were self-destructive acts in the form of substance abuse and extramarital affairs. Restin sought unconsciously to maintain this personal self-belief and to reenact the self-destructive role in marriage. In like manner, Sue unconsciously cooperated with Restin in order to maintain her personal mythology and to reenact her family of origin role. Her personal mythology included the belief that her personal needs were secondary to others' needs and that she had no right to expect any joy and satisfaction in life. She believed her role was to take on the job of caring for others even when they were adult and could and should take care of themselves.

Restin and Sue's unconscious marital mythology centered on the expectation that the ideal mate would preserve and maintain one's position in the family of origin. They did not disappoint each other. Restin needed someone to take care of him and to maintain his self-image as an irresponsible child, and Sue needed an irresponsible child for whom to care. In this sense there was a hand-to-glove fit in their ideal mate expectation. However, this fit was dysfunctional and contributed to preserving unhealthy and un-nurturing personal mythologies. Nor could the marital mythology nurture them in positive ways. It only contributed to their further frustration.

Although Restin and Sue had an unconscious contractual collusion, they still had expectations of an ideal mate that transcended their neurotic marital contract. Each desired to have his or her emotional needs met. Each looked to the other for validation of his or her basic worth as a human being. Each wanted the other to bolster self-esteem. Each looked to the other to care for him or her in time of need. Finally, each needed his or her emotional heart hungers met through mutual sharing and mutual support. These unfulfilled needs were what each brought to marital therapy. However, these same needs were overridden by the unconscious neurotic contract, which demanded that both put aside and sacrifice these needs in order to maintain their family of origin roles.

Counseling was initiated when Sue decided that she did not want to live by the neurotic contract any longer. Restin agreed to come to counseling only because he knew Sue was serious. However, his unconscious goal in counseling was to keep the original contract in place. My goal as counselor was to help Sue explore her dissatisfaction in the marriage and work to overcome her need to keep Restin a child. My goal with Restin was to support him as he attempted to take responsibility for his own life and to confront his efforts to manipulate Sue into the old marital contract.

My goals were identified, and Sue confirmed that her goal was similar to my goal for her. Restin agreed that he wanted his life to be better, but he expressed pessimism about any possibility of change if God did not work a miracle.

Before going farther in the analysis of the case, it may be helpful to reflect on how addiction and co-dependency interrelate in developing a marital mythology.

Marital Mythology, Addiction, and Co-dependency

Addiction is defined as a person's attachment to something on which he or she depends for satisfaction and for which the person is willing to sacrifice everything else.[5] Sources of satisfaction include substances (drugs, alcohol, nicotine, caffeine, sugar) and behavioral patterns (in regard to social and sexual relationships, spending, gambling, working, practicing religion, watching television, eating, exercising, and wielding power). People suffering from addiction often come from dysfunctional families of origin. In addition, these persons tend to be dependent on others and look to others to fix them. They also have excessive guilt feelings and feelings of powerlessness. They are usually dishonest and self-centered.

Persons with addictions have certain beliefs that make up their personal mythologies. There are commonly at least five such beliefs. The first belief is the conviction of unlovability, and the second is the feeling that one is completely worthless. The certainty that one is beyond hope and help and the certainty that one's addiction is more important than family, friends, work, or values constitute the third and fourth beliefs. The final assumption is that one is condemned to the place of the despicable because of the addiction. In order for addiction to take hold there has to be a co-dependent environment. A co-dependent is a person who assumes responsibility for other people's behavior and attempts to deal with his or her own pain by controlling others.[6] These persons come from bonding relationships forged with addicted persons, and they enter into a toxic pact with the addicted person. Co-dependents, like addicts, are often adult children of dysfunctional families and many of them continue to play the caretaking role learned in the family of origin. The co-dependent suffers from deep unmet needs similar to the needs of the addict; however, the co-dependent became a caretaker rather than an addict.

The personal mythology of the co-dependent person consists of the following beliefs.[7] There is a belief that one's self-worth and appearance are defective. The person also concludes that he or she is trapped in life and responds by becoming a victim and martyr. The person is convinced that the only way to live is by serving others; however, this serving is self-demeaning and self-destructive. There are many feelings including guilt about not doing enough. Consequently, a co-dependent person is always exhausted. He or she is locked into this pattern because he or she believes that survival itself depends on carrying out the caretaking role.

A co-dependent person also uses certain psychological defenses to maintain the co-dependent pattern.[8] Co-dependents often deny their own feelings, and interpret the behavior of others in distorted ways. There is often a dissociation or separation from one's own feelings that makes it difficult for the co-dependent to deal with reality. There is a compulsive need to separate the self from anxiety related to guilt and shame by overworking and serving. Not being in relationship to an addict often produces unbearable anxiety, which is the result of a belief in a flawed self. A co-dependent relationship may be the only relationship a co-dependent can tolerate. This promotes a co-dependent environment.

Restin and Sue came from dysfunctional families, and they brought to the marriage negative personal mythologies. Emotionally, they needed each other, and their relationship produced a negative marital mythology. They entered into an addictive and co-dependent relationship where each person could maintain his or her own personal mythology—a neurotic pact where they unconsciously agreed to preserve each other's family of origin pathology. Because each still had hope that each would find the ideal mate who would rescue him or her from the other's predicament, neither was satisfied with the mate. Each brought complaints to pastoral counseling. Both had severe unmet needs that were distorted because of each spouse's personal mythology.

Both Restin and Sue had found Bible stories that challenged the way they had irrationally entered into an unhealthy marital contract. Through pastoral counseling and the use of Bible stories, there was a dynamic at work that could dethrone their neurotic marital mythology.

SIGNIFICANT BIBLE STORIES

We have said that the role of the biblical story is often to draw the reader or hearer into itself through its attracting power. This alluring power of Scripture and the role-taking tendency of the Bible reader facilitate counselees' identification with certain characters, situations, and plots that hold out potential for change. Note Sue's identification with Bible stories.

P.C.: I have been spending a lot of time with Restin and the stories with which he identifies. Are there stories that you identify with in your present situation?

Sue: Restin and I have been talking about this lately. As we talked we both came to the awareness that the story of Martha and Mary fits my situation.

P.C.: With whom did you identify?

Sue: I feel embarrassed to say this, but Martha seems to fit my situation very well.

P.C.: Explain that to me.

Sue: Well, it seems like I spend my time worrying about things I can't control. I spend my time working hard and I can't enjoy my life.

Sue identified with the biblical narrative in Luke 10:38-42. This is a story of two sisters, Mary and Martha, who knew Jesus and had invited him to their home. Martha received Jesus and offered hospitality to him. She spent her time preparing for the visit once Jesus had arrived. Mary did not engage in the preparation of hospitality; instead, she sat at the feet of Jesus listening to his teaching and taking it all in. Martha was frustrated and upset because she was working while Mary was not. Martha asked Jesus to dismiss Mary so that she could also engage in helping. Jesus took the opportunity to point out to Martha how anxious and troubled she appeared. Jesus also defended Mary by saying that she had chosen to do the right thing, and the results of what she had heard could not be taken from her.

Sue saw a parallel between her life and that of Martha. How accurate was Sue's identification with Martha from a biblical narrative critical point of view?

From a narrative critical point of view, it is important first to put this story in the context of other stories in Luke 10. This story is only one episode narrated in this chapter. Other narrations include the mission of the seventy, who were sent out to heal the sick and to proclaim the nearness of the kingdom of God in verse 9. Another narrative is the story of the good Samaritan, where Jesus taught what it meant to be a good neighbor. The story of Martha and Mary follows the good Samaritan story. The context of the story, then, is a sequence where Jesus is teaching and preaching about the kingdom or rule of God. From this brief contextualization of the story, it is possible to conclude that the narrator in Luke 10 was concerned about the kingdom of God. Perhaps this story is about challenging Martha to look beyond her immediate anxiety and worries and toward the coming of the kingdom of God that was present in Jesus.

An analysis of the story in light of literary protocol is instructive, for it focuses on how the narrator introduces the characters in a story to achieve a certain impact on the reader or hearer.[9] One protocol involves introducing a character who has desirable traits that the narrator wants those who hear the story to adopt. Then the narrator introduces a second character who has the opposite traits that should not be adopted. The skill of the narrator is to include in the narration the consequences for adopting the traits of the characters.

In the story of Mary and Martha, the audience is drawn to identify with both Mary and Martha. Martha was shown to possess traits that were the result of anxiety and worry. Mary, on the other hand, was portrayed as a person who could relax and who could take advantage of the opportunities that were presented to her. The consequence for Martha was a reprimand from Jesus, and the consequence for Mary was support for her openness and readiness. The narrator is obviously trying to convey to the audience what was important and had priority in the moment. Martha was concerned about controlling the moment and Mary was concerned to hear the wisdom that Jesus was sharing. Perhaps the narrator is concerned to show what character traits were needed when the kingdom was close at hand.

Sue felt drawn to both characters through the alluring power of the story and because of her role-taking tendencies. She found that the story pinpointed her main problem of co-dependency. She was able to see that she needed to come to grips with her own pattern of overfunctioning as a caretaker. She used this story to bring sanction to the possibility that God was moving her in a different direction. For a long time she had felt that her service was God's will. However, she began to consider that she might not be doing God's will after all. As a result, this story became a chief means for her to reflect on her caretaking patterns.

Sue made the connection to this story herself. Given the literary analysis, her identification was very appropriate.

Sue: I can get so busy that I don't have time to really concentrate on my needs. I feel like I have neglected myself all these years in order to care for Restin. I am not only getting tired, I also may be messing up my life spiritually.

P.C.:   Messing up your life spiritually?

Sue: I have been reading books on co-dependency. I really participate in keeping Restin like he is. I am working very hard now to stop doing things he should be doing for himself. Because I spend so much time taking care of him, I am neglecting my spiritual well-being. I am now coming to a better understanding that I have a distorted view of my Christian duty. I am realizing that self-sacrifice might not be the best thing spiritually. Mary had learned the appropriate lesson, and Jesus was trying to teach Martha how to relax and enjoy the savior's presence.

P.C.: Looks like this story has caused you to think real deeply about your relationship with Restin and with God.

Sue: It sure has.

Sue went on to talk about her role in relationship to Restin's addiction, and she also said she felt convicted by the story. She began to see that her co-dependency was standing in the way of her relationship with God and her achieving a healthy self.

Recall that Restin and Sue's marital mythology related to two concerns, (1) the neurotic contract and (2) the ideal mate expectations. Sue saw immediately the relationship between her co-dependency and the Martha and Mary story. She knew that she needed help in not contributing to the addiction of Restin. She also knew that she must find ways to make her needs primary and not to sacrifice them as she had been doing. Consequently, working toward changing her personal mythology would have direct impact on the marital mythology. Her goal was to separate herself from the neurotic contract.

Although she was aware of the co-dependency, Sue was not aware of her ideal mate expectations. She was aware that the marital relationship was not very fulfilling, but she did not know what she could realistically expect from the marital relationship. She did realize, however, that she was responsible for making her own life meaningful even if she could not expect very much from the marital relationship.

Restin actively resisted Sue's withdrawing from the neurotic contract. When he realized that she was serious about it, he had to begin to think about how he was going to live his life without someone to take care of him. This forced him not only to deal with the neurotic contract, but also to begin to revise his expectations of the ideal mate. He still wanted someone to be his caretaker, however.

In the exploration of his unwillingness to give up the neurotic contract and his insistence on being taken care of, he said that perhaps he was like those "stiff-necked" people. He was saying this in jest, and I felt he was trying to express his anger at me for pushing in this area. He was just responding with whatever came to his mind. However, I explored with him what this metaphor of being stiff-necked meant.

Since he liked Bible stories and liked to tell them to me, he began to tell the story of the "stiff-necked" people in Exodus 33:3, 5. This story picked up on the wilderness theme, to which we continually returned throughout our counseling time together.

It is important to take a narrative look at Exodus 33:3 and 5 for background information on why this passage became important in dismantling Restin's unhealthy personal and marital mythology.

> Go up to a land flowing with milk and honey; but I will not go up among you, or I would consume you on the way, for you are a stiff-necked people. (33:3)
>
> For the LORD had said to Moses, "Say to the Israelites, 'You are a stiff-necked people; if for a single moment I should go up among you, I would consume you. So now take off your ornaments, and I will decide what to do to you.'" (33:5)

The book of Exodus was a narrative used by a faith community in exile, and it is because of the Exile that it has appeal. The audience that heard the story would have been concerned for deliverance, forgiveness, divine presence, and absence.[10] The same concern would exist today according to Terrence Fretheim. He says:

> For centuries the exodus has functioned as a paradigm especially for those who have been victimized by oppressive systems of one kind or another. God is the champion of the poor and those pushed to the margins of life; God is one who liberates them

from the pharaohs of this world. As God acted then, so God can be expected to act again. In the United States, Negro spirituals have carried on these Exodus themes, and Black Theology is permeated with them.[11]

Once the narrator got the attention of the reader or hearer, the story sought to draw the people into itself to do specific things. What would identification with stiff-necked people mean to those who first heard the story? The narrator was trying to convey to the audience that there was a failure in faith and that they had forgotten that God had brought them out of bondage. Moreover, the narrator was telling them that they had a significant role to play in God's salvation drama, and this role was threatened by their insistence on following idols.[12]

The naivete of the Israelites was significant. They did not bargain with the wilderness wanderings being so difficult. It was a surprise to them. "Instead of a land of milk and honey, they get a desert."[13] They felt the promise had fallen short and that God had forsaken them in the wilderness. "Salvation from one death leads into the teeth of another."[14]

These were the exact feelings of Restin. He felt that his recovery from addiction should not have led him toward having to be responsible for his life. He felt entitled to live his life without demands, and he did not want to assume this responsibility. He literally saw himself like the Israelites, and he did not want to learn the lessons of the wilderness. He had no desire to learn his vocation in God's salvation drama and thought the pain of his earlier life entitled him to be exempt from any further pain or risk. Our counseling spent many hours on the wilderness experience and what life realistically had to offer. The counseling focused on his resistance to accepting the work that was moving him from addiction into service.

The Exodus narrative of the stiff-necked people was helping Restin to claim his role in God's salvation drama as well as helping him to claim the responsibility for his own behavior and life.

It was in this claiming that his personal and marital mythology were being addressed simultaneously. To embrace the story and its implications would mean that Restin would renounce his negative personal mythology and the neurotic marital contract. It would mean that he would assume more responsibility for his life and for his behavior in the marriage. It would mean that he would have to see himself differently and make contributions to the welfare of others.

There were indeed hopeful stories at work challenging the personal mythologies and marital mythology of Sue and Restin. Making them aware of these dynamic stories and the implications for their lives was part of the re-authoring process. Prior to turning to this process, it is important to explore the role-taking tendencies of both Restin and Sue.

Story Identification and Construing Reality

Role-taking theory is applicable in this case. Both Sue and Restin were predisposed to identifying with Bible stories and characters because of their religious backgrounds. They both identified with specific Bible stories and characters that helped to bring perspective to their lives. From these stories and characters, they learned to come to expect certain things to happen in their lives, and they also began to interpret their lives in light of these stories.

Role-taking did have an influence on Sue's and Restin's lives. How the Bible stories addressed their marital mythology has already been recounted. It is also important to explore how these stories influenced what they expected from life.

Identification with Bible stories frequently stimulates the expectation that the Bible reader will be treated in a manner similar to that of Bible characters. Often, the identification produces what can be called expectation of possibility. This refers to hopeful alternatives to the current way of construing reality and handling problems. Such hopeful alternatives include envisaging the problem facing the Bible reader as manageable. If the problem is viewed as manageable, it can be confronted with optimism. The second expectation of possibility relates to a conviction that one is not alone in facing the problem, that others are there to give support. A third expectation of possibility is the belief that the way of construing reality holds out new and novel alternatives to the construal already in operation.[15]

From the perspective of role-taking, identification with Bible stories and characters holds out these three expectations of possibility. For example, when Restin and Sue identified with their respective Bible stories, role-theory would suggest that they would take on certain expectations about their situation in life. Restin's identification with "stiff-necked" people would bring with it construing the outcome of his condition in predictable ways. By taking on the role of the "stiff-necked," he would begin to envisage the outcome of his predicament as tragic. Consequently, the hopeful possibility was in changing his attitude. The story would also indicate he was not alone, in that God would accompany him in making the change in attitude. Making the change in attitude would also mean that he could actualize new and novel solutions to his problem.

Sue could derive similar benefits by role-taking with Martha. According to the theory, her identification with the story brought with it the expectation that her problem was manageable. It also conveyed that she was not alone in facing her predicament, since Jesus was her companion. If she could face the problem and deal with her Martha tendencies, she could expect changes in her life.

These two stories with which Sue and Restin identified influenced them in the three ways just outlined. They both began to construe their problems of addiction and co-dependency in different and in hopeful ways. They knew that they were not alone in facing their problems and that there was hope for new behavior and attitudes in the future.

A big problem remained an obstacle for both of them, however. Their religious environment and their role-taking heritage led to some unrealistic expectations along with the positive expectations. They were taught a blind triumphal vision of divine help in their religious heritage, and to expect that their lives would conform exactly to the Bible story. Consequently, when Restin began to try to change from being "stiff-necked" and when Sue tried to be more like Mary than Martha, they expected immediate transformation in their lives. They did not realize that their attempts would take them down a complex path and involve a long process of transformation. They expected sudden changes in their lives. When the sudden changes did not occur, a crisis of faith resulted.

These triumphalist expectations became therapeutic issues for both Sue and Restin. One way that I sought to handle the expectations was to emphasize that a narrative perspective undergirded many of the stories of the Bible. This meant that when viewed as a whole, the stories in the Bible were episodes in the unfolding of the kingdom of God, which involved a process in time. Consequently, the emphasis moved to the fact that Martha's change must be viewed in light of the complete unfolding of the salvation drama. This meant that miracles that Jesus performed were in a series that pointed beyond themselves to the transformation of the given order of reality. This transformation of reality was begun by Jesus and continues today. It is not completed. Therefore, Bible stories should be seen as pieces to the unfolding kingdom rather than as pointing to the sudden and miraculous. With Restin, the emphasis on process was a little easier to convey, because the Israelites' transformation from "stiff-necked" to obedient required forty years.

Role-taking with Bible stories is accompanied by new expectations and hoped for possibilities. When naive triumphalist expectations become problematical, they can be addressed in pastoral counseling by emphasizing the narrative perspective of the unfolding drama of the kingdom that undergirds the entire Scripture. Viewing personal transformation in light of an unfolding drama facilitates the process of using the Bible in pastoral counseling. It helps people to develop a hopeful perspective that is realistic and consistent with Scripture. Pastoral counseling then becomes a means of monitoring personal transformation in terms of an unfolding, thickening, and twisting plot. This means that personal change is complex, and it includes reversals as well as progress toward the desired end.

Sue and Restin began to learn that the changes in their lives would take time, and they would have to develop tolerance and patience for their shortcomings. This was a constant struggle for them, given their religious backgrounds. However, their struggles were hopeful, because they were aware that significant changes were occurring in them even though these changes were slow.

THE RE-AUTHORING PROCESS

The purpose of the re-authoring process is to gain distance from the presenting problem and to identify hopeful alternatives that can be pursued in counseling. Both Sue and Restin had identified their problem and the hopeful alternatives that were at work in their lives challenging their personal and marital mythologies.

Identifying the problem and hopeful alternatives is just the beginning of counseling. The patterns of addiction and co-dependency are very difficult to overcome. In addition to therapy, both Restin and Sue required the kind of support that came from narcotics and co-dependence support programs. I helped them to work through the patterns of resistance and the fears associated with changing lifelong patterns. However, there needed to be the support of "like others" to keep them motivated and working.

Throughout my work with both Sue and Restin, we turned continually to Bible stories that were at work in their lives. We reflected on the stories and their implications for the problems raised in the counseling sessions. I found them not only effective handles for keeping a clear focus, but also an important source of motivation.

CHAPTER FIVE

FAMILY MYTHOLOGY AND GRIEVING FOR A CHILD

T his chapter explores the role of Bible stories in challenging negative family mythologies. The focus is on how unresolved marital problems and their consequent family mythology had a tragic consequence for the lives of several children. The role of the Bible is examined at critical junctures in the development of marriage and family life of a particular family—that of Delores and Will, first mentioned briefly in the Preface. The use of Scripture was evident at four critical periods in the lives of this family: (1) coming to grips with the loss of their youngest son, (2) overcoming many wounds and hurts from the past, (3) facilitating growth and transformation, and (4) interpreting and reinterpreting life in the midst of tragedy.

In order to reintroduce the family, I want to begin with a testimony of Delores, the wife and mother, written after her loss of a son and after several years of family counseling. This testimony was published in *Gospel Herald* and *The Sunday School Times*.[1]

My Favorite Bible Text

"Oh, no!" I cried, hoping to just faint away. I wanted to wake up later and find it all had been just a nightmare.

Unconsciousness did not shield me, however. I felt firm hands reaching out and gripping me. I was escorted to a couch.

Someone asked whether I wanted a cup of water. I said yes. Uncontrolled tears returned as I remembered the sad sight of my young son, Jeremiah Samuel. He was in a hospital bed, swollen and comatose and connected to a life-support machine.

An hour earlier Sam and his older brother, Willie Leneil, were playing in the bathtub, watching an imaginary waterfall descend into the drain.

Feeling comfortable about their playing together, I had decided to go write a quick business letter. I recall hearing the children chattering and playing. A moment later I became absorbed with the letter. After finishing the first draft, I was about to quickly rewrite it but thought, I must check on the children.

I perked up my ears and listened intently. Strangely, I heard only the sound of rushing water. In the grip of fear, I ran into the bathroom and saw Sam floating face down. Will was attempting to get out of the tub. When I looked at the drain, I saw that a red plastic toy was blocking it.

At the hospital emergency room, the doctors insisted that I call my husband. They would then discuss the situation, with us both present. Friends arrived, and we began praying. We hugged and shed tears.

After my husband arrived, the doctors told us that our son was in critical condition. They would do all they could. They encouraged us to pray, saying maybe that would help.

Before this crisis, I do not recall praying so much in my life. It seemed that with almost each passing second, I would send up another intercessory prayer for Sam to God. On my knees and with each caress, I prayed for Sam. For two weeks I begged God for mercy.

I could not bear to leave Sam's side, and every moment I would hold him up in prayer. I could not bear the thought of my prayers for him being interrupted.

After finding that Sam had minimal brain-wave activity, the doctors told us he was legally brain-dead. They wanted to disconnect him from the respirator. My husband passively agreed, but I would not. My first reaction was that I never would let them disconnect Sam from his only hope for life.

My professor and pastoral counselor, Dr. Edward Wimberly,

finally convinced me to let Sam be taken off the machine and placed in God's hands. God would make the final decision. Dr. Wimberly held my hand as they disconnected the machine. Sam was pronounced dead.

In the initial period of grief and guilt, I did not know what to say to God; I did not understand what He was saying to me. The only reality was that Sam was dead.

After Sam's funeral, I began contemplating again how I should proceed in prayer. I had to face the fact that I would never hold Sam again. I thought, maybe God had not helped me out of the crisis the way I wanted Him to; I would let Him down by hanging up in my prayer life.

I decided to continue hoping in the Lord despite the circumstances, however. I realized that without the Lord, I could not be the person I should be.

I approached God with an honest prayer like this one: "God, are there no miracles for me? My hands, ears, and judgment slipped for a second; and death filled in all too quickly. God, I thought I was a new creature in Christ; how, then, could I still err in my way? Lord, love him for me."

As I continued talking to God in honest prayer, I was inwardly encouraged to spend a lot of time reading Scripture. I soon encountered Psalm 86, which proved to be filled with ministering words of life for my situation.

I read, "Bow down thine ear, O LORD, hear me: for I am poor and needy" (Psalm 86:1 KJV). This verse helped me respond to God. I felt that I did not have to come up to God with words. I did not feel that God would bow down His ear to me. I was empty and in need of the provisions of the Lord.

I also read, "Preserve my soul; for I am holy: O thou my God, save thy servant that trusteth in thee" (Psalm 86:2 KJV). I remembered the first joy of being born again.

I could feel the hope of God preserving my soul even through the fires of grief and guilt. I believe that I knew the guilt and grief would be too much to bear, and so I had another reason for asking the Lord to preserve my soul and to help me through the times of the dark nights and the trying of my soul.

Because of this verse, I could relinquish the guilt of losing a child through negligence, which was like a broiling fire. I was reassured that even in this fire, God could meet my needs.

It is ironic that the doctors said prayers would help. My spiritual life is not the same as it was before the accident. Within the past three years, I have matured into a Christian who starts and ends each day with prayer and devotion. I now consult the Word of God all day long. I know prayers helped me. I have learned from experience that God is faithful to His promise to be with us always. God was with me and helped me through the grief and the guilt.

God has shown me "a token for good; that they which hate me may see it, and be ashamed: because thou, LORD, hast [helped] me, and comforted me" (Psalm 86:17 KJV).

From God I have received the greatest gifts in the world—salvation and the Holy Spirit, who is the Comforter.

(John 14:16-17)

This is a testimony that comes at the end of a four-year struggle that began long before Sam's death. I was involved with them as a family counselor for a long period of time, and I have watched their pilgrimage with God and how God has used a variety of vehicles to revise their personal, marital, and family mythologies in ways that have made them better persons, better spouses, and better parents. Through their own growth and development, my life has been much enriched.

Delores sent me her testimony in the mail at the time I was working on the second draft of this manuscript. I did not have in mind who I would focus on for this chapter, but the idea to share this family's experience surfaced as soon as I read Delores' article.

Since they have been identified because of Delores' published testimony, I have sought their permission to use the article as well as their counsel on the content for this chapter. They know my aim is to suggest how God's work through the Scriptures has assisted people in overcoming negative personal, marital, and family mythologies.

ASSESSMENT OF FAMILY MYTHOLOGY

From the very beginning of counseling, both Will and Delores sought to interpret and reinterpret their experiences in light of Scripture. Being African Americans who had grown up in the black church, they held a fondness for Scripture and its practical usefulness for living. Consequently, it was very easy for me to promote their use of Scripture as well as the Scripture's potential to challenge the negative mythologies in their lives.

At the time of my pastoral counseling with them, I had not developed the theory of narrative psychology and the rhetorical uses of Scripture. However, when I turned to my notes on every session, I became aware that a use of the Bible in pastoral theology similar to the system advocated here was operative during at least the preceding four years of my clinical practice. I probably learned how to use the Bible in pastoral counseling and care and in pastoral theology from people like Delores and Will.

Bagarozzi and Anderson point out that each spouse brings to the marriage his or her ideal cognitive representation of each child that is born into the family.[2] Like the marital mythology, these ideal child images often change when emotionally mature parents encounter the actual child. Conversely, parents who are less emotionally mature find ways to get the child to conform to their ideal child image regardless of the child's developmental and emotional needs and interests.

It is also pointed out by Bagarozzi and Anderson that unresolved conflicts from the parents' own personal mythologies are often reactivated by a child who is facing certain developmental tasks. This often happens when the child begins to face certain developmental tasks that one or both parents may have failed to resolve earlier in their lives. In this case, the child and the parents' personal mythology will begin to clash.

Another source of conflict comes when the child is assigned a role that belongs to the grandparents. This is called irrational role assignment; the ideal child is asked to reverse roles with the parents.[3] This blurs the boundaries between generations.[4] In the blurring of generational boundaries, or in the irrational assignment of roles, the child is often coerced to conform to the ideal child image held by the parents.

With Will and Delores, whatever ideal child images they had brought into the marriage were permanently disrupted by the death of Sam. His death put both parents deeply in touch with what it meant to be parents, and how parental and spousal relationships were intertwined. The shock of Sam's death forced them to attend to issues of their marital mythology and child rearing with urgency. They knew that their remaining son needed their full attention and priority as they went about other tasks. There was no need to uncover the various levels of mythology, because they were well engaged in this process as part of their grief process.

As Delores indicated, the death of Sam was a tragic accident resulting from a moment of negligence, and this negligence was related to the demands of being a graduate student overwhelmed with school, being a mother, and being a wife. Sam's death was not affecting the personal, marital, or family mythology so far as I could tell. However, the personal, marital, and family mythologies surfaced and were involved in the process of healing.

THE GRIEVING PROCESS

Grief—or the process of giving up the lost loved one and emancipating the self from bondage to the deceased—was the first task in our family counseling together. The grief process is accomplished by reviewing one's relationship to the deceased and expressing feelings of loss, abandonment, and guilt. Often complaints to God and desire for God to have intervened and performed a miracle are part of the process of grieving. This is also a time of bargaining with God where one promises to do extra work for God if God will just reverse what has happened. Moreover, losing a child through negligence made the grieving process even harder for both Delores and Will.

Of striking significance to me was Will's support of Delores. At no time did he blame her for what had happened. When I explored his reason, he said he had already sensed that something tragic was going to happen in his family. He explained he had given over most of the caretaking chores to his wife and was very busy making a living for the family. He said he had had a strange dream where he wrestled all night with the devil. He called it a "real fight" and said he had awoke sweating. Will indicated he had realized then that he had to change his priorities and assist Delores more with the two boys.

This dream took place two weeks prior to the death of Sam. As a result, Will resolved to come closer to his family to protect it from danger. He had anticipated a tragedy, and though he commented he had had no idea it would be as severe as it was, when he received the call to come to the hospital he "knew" that something evil had struck his family.

I was surprised and greatly encouraged by his unwavering support of Delores and how he was able to own his role in the unfortunate turn of events. They grieved together and supported each other and their remaining son in remarkable ways throughout the grief process.

Although it would become important to them later, I had not yet heard Delores make reference to Psalm 86 during the entire counseling process, though both Will and Delores used other biblical material in their grieving. One biblical story that surfaced was the story of David. He mourned the loss of the son that was born out of the sin of adultery with Bathsheba prior to the murder of Uriah the Hittite in 2 Samuel 11:1-4. Delores talked about 2 Samuel 12:13-23, where the prophet Nathan told David that his sinful deed was forgiven, but because of the scorn of God, the child born to that unholy union would die. David and Bathsheba's son grew sick and later died. He very much wanted this child to remain alive, but it did die, and David was very hurt. By the time the child was born, David had married Bathsheba, and when the child died Bathsheba conceived Solomon (2 Samuel 12:24).

Delores found David's desire to keep his son alive very similar to her experience. When the child died, David expressed his grief and turned back to God's service. Delores said that this story helped her express her real grief and desire for her son, but she was going to pattern her life after David's and give up her son to God and return to living.

At the session in which Delores identified with this story and told of how she was working through her grief, she also expressed a desire that Will could express his grief. She said she realized that he was grieving too but that he was doing it silently. She said she wished he could be like her and express it more openly in their relationship. It was at this point that he told his story of how he had had a dream where he was attacked by Satan. He said that as part of his means of combating Satan, Psalm 23 had come to him and he had recited it word for word. He indicated that up to that point he had never recited the twenty-third psalm. He said the words came to him as if he had cited it all his life. Through Will's brief confession, they both felt in solidarity with each other.

I don't really know if Delores' reference to Psalm 86 in her article related precisely to the exact period in her life when she was working with the grief over the loss of her son. However, I believe that Psalm 86 takes on special meaning in light of Delores' recounting the story of David's loss of his son. I believe that this psalm captures the depth of feeling that both David and Delores were experiencing. Psalm 86 is categorized as an individual lament, and it relates to individuals who faced initial shock over tragedy.[5] It was obvious from Delores' use of the psalm that the psalm enabled her to enter into a helpful relationship with God and express her profound feelings of loss. This psalm facilitated her ability to come to grips with grief.

Donald Capps talks about the functions of psalms of lament in facilitating the grief process in *Biblical Approaches to Pastoral Counseling*.[6] One of the significant things that he does in this book is to relate the form of the psalms of lament to the stages of the grief process.[7] He points out that one of the functions of the psalms of lament is to rehabilitate and restore those who are suffering.[8] The lament defines the suffering and tells the sufferer the correct form in which the lament is to be experienced. It also shapes how the one experiencing grief feels and expresses feelings appropriately for healing. It facilitates the expression of deep emotions of hurt, guilt, and anger, and at the same time draws the sufferer closer to God. Consequently, at the end of the psalm the sufferer feels healed.

Psalm 23 played a similar role in Will's grief. Psalm 23 is an individual psalm of trust with a lament.[9] The psalm gave Will the trust that God was with him and would hold him up in the time of difficulty and fear. It enabled him not only to grieve but to be confident in the face of the attack from evil.

There was a real similarity between the grieving of David and Delores. The following excerpt from a counseling session gives some clues to how biblical narrative was at work in the grieving process of Delores.

Delores: I got angry with you another time.

P.C.: You didn't let me know.

Delores: I didn't have to. God has been dealing with my attitude.

P.C.: Give me an example.

Delores: At this moment I am learning about my self-righteousness. I have been discovering that there is a lot of things God is doing with me. This is why I get mad at you; you make me think of things that are uncomfortable for me.

P.C.: Give me an example of what God is doing with you.

Delores: Have you ever experienced God being for you no matter what you have done? This can make you self-righteous. Then, God teaches you that it is grace that is at work. Therefore, I have no reason to be self-righteous. Look at me and what happened to Sam. This is off the subject, but someone said I killed Sam. I have to deal with this. At first I felt depressed; then, I felt at peace. You asked me whether I had mourned Sam. This is another reason I get mad at you. You raise issues that hurt. Yes, I mourn Sam. David mourned his child. So what is wrong with me mourning my child?

P.C.: Tell me about King David. I don't remember that part of the story.

Delores: (With surprise in her voice) You don't remember? It's in the Bible. You should know that story.

P.C.: Thank you.

Delores: O.K. It is in 2 Samuel in the twelfth chapter. It is right here. [She gets out her Bible.] He was fasting, praying, and mourning, and the child died. It was in the twenty-second verse. He said: "While the child was still alive, I fasted and wept. Who knows: The Lord may be gracious to me, and the child may live. But, now he is dead; why should I fast? Can I bring him back again? I shall go to him, but he will not return to me." And you asked me was I going to him.

P.C.: When did I ask that?

Delores: Forget about that. This is why I have to do what God wants me to do even if I feel like a fool. When that person said to me what he did, I felt like I wanted to die. Now I have experienced God's peace. I was not going to die. God really has come through for me.

In this brief interview excerpt, Delores is exploring her grief and how the Bible story of David's grief over his son helps her to come to grips with the loss of Sam and her tremendous guilt. She felt guilt and blame for the loss, but this story helped her to experience God's peace. She was a bit uncomfortable with God's care of her and worried about being self-righteous. Yet, she knew God was at work in her.

The ideal child image that preceded the death of Sam is important to address in light of this interview. I was struck by the naming of Sam. Sam was born at a time when Delores and Will were in turmoil. I think that Sam had a great deal of significance for them because of the marital conflict. Will had distanced himself from the family in his work. For comfort in his absence and when things were difficult between them, Delores relied a great deal on mothering her children. The name Samuel had biblical significance for her; it made Sam special. It seemed to me that he existed to save their marriage. Both of them reacted as if he had died so that they might have new life. Delores especially felt very guilty for this; consequently, for God to forgive her was the greatest thing that could have happened to her. God's love of her gave her peace because she felt terribly guilty that she had let someone she cherished die.

Sam and little Will both seemed to be the glue that held them together. For a time the children were the saviors of their marriage. However, it was difficult for them to come together as husband and wife without seeing the children primarily in that light. As a result, the children's own needs seemed secondary to their marital needs.

I also realized that both had aspirations for ministry and that Delores was actually engaged in pursuing a seminary degree at the time of Sam's death. It was only during the grieving process that it became apparent that Will also had aspirations for ministry. Whatever ideal child images they had, the death of Sam almost immediately caused them to revise all the myths that they brought to the family. The biblical material helped them to confront the real circumstances of their relationship and of their individual hang-ups. It caused them to revise their expectations of each other and of their remaining child in light of the real situation. They revised their priorities as husband and wife and as parents. They made their relationship with each other primary, and this was closely followed by rearing their remaining son based on his needs rather than on their own needs. They began to acquire age-appropriate child-rearing skills, to work out mutual caregiving roles, and to plan how they both were going to achieve their ministerial aspirations in mutual ways that did not neglect their parenting role or the spousal relationship.

One real danger was that both Will and Delores could have been overcome by blame. Delores especially could have felt that she was a negligent parent and taken on the belief in herself as an ineffectual and incompetent parent. Will could have believed that he was a neglectful and incompetent father who paid more attention to his work and career than to his family. However, the biblical resources helped them face the truth about themselves as well as turn around their lives to meet the demands of the situation. Rather than develop negative mythologies about their personal lives and their married and family life, they were able to develop nurturing mythologies that have sustained their lives ever since the death of Sam, more than four years ago. Scripture played a significant role in their ability to forge new and healthy mythologies in the face of tragedy.

OVERCOMING WOUNDS FROM THE PAST

One of the sources of personal conflict for Delores was her distrust of authority figures in her life. This surfaced one day when she became aware that she had unresolved business with her family of origin. She had witnessed something in her parents' relationship that she felt she had to confront with her parents. Clearly, she had been carrying around some pain and felt a great deal of anger toward her husband, her in-laws, and her own family that was the result of this unfinished business.

Delores found it very difficult to forgive those who hurt and shamed her in her past. She viewed all her relationships in light of the past wounds. When she saw how her anger over the past was preventing her from dealing with the present, she was able to return to the past for the purposes of healing. She came to grips with the need to talk to each parent about these concerns, and this freed her from some of the baggage that she brought to the marriage.

Two scriptures surfaced during this period of Delores' self-reflection. She talked about Psalm 15:3 and 2 Corinthians 12:10. The psalm verse reads, "Who does not slander with his tongue, and does no evil to his friend, nor takes up a reproach against his neighbor" (RSV). She saw this psalm as an opportunity to acknowledge how she had indiscriminately expressed her rage and anger toward others rather than deal with its source and pain within her family of origin. She was able to recognize how this anger affected her married life and hindered achievement of her goals. She also acknowledged that the source of her anger had to do with unresolved issues that related more to her mother than it did to her father.

So the psalm functioned to help her to own her anger. Commonly, the function of a psalm is not only to help persons be aware of their shortcomings but also to help persons accept themselves despite the shortcomings.[10] Second Corinthians 12:10 also assisted this process of acceptance. This is the Scripture where Paul talks of his thorn in the flesh and how the power of God sustained him despite his weakness. She interpreted this Scripture to mean that she could accept this negative side of herself without beating herself for not being perfect. She found a profound sense of acceptance despite her limitations.

Will saw the growth in Delores' self-acceptance, and this aided him in accepting his own limitations as well as his strengths. During this time he accepted his call to ministry and began his preparation for ministry. He said that he had previously denied his call and let Delores accept the call for them both, but he was now beginning to realize that he had to accept responsibility for his own call.

The fact that Scripture had healing power for them has been illustrated. When either of them grew as individuals, the family grew. Certain personal beliefs about themselves that were not accurate were challenged by Scripture, and Scripture enabled them to accept themselves even with their imperfections. Grace was truly administered through these stories and Scriptures. Pastoral counseling became the context in which the stories and Scripture did their healing work on negative mythologies and supported the development of positive mythologies.

GROWTH, TRANSFORMATION, AND PARENTING

The growth and transformation of Will and Delores did benefit their parenting roles. Part of the concern of the pastoral counseling was for the health and well-being of little Will, and therefore he attended the family counseling sessions. He was too young to really participate verbally, but it was interesting to see how his other ways of participation depended on the level of anxiety in the room. When the tension in his parents' relationship was evident, little Will would leave his drawings and his toys and come closer to his parents. If the anxiety increased, he would directly intervene by disrupting the counseling. However, when Will and Delores were actually cooperating with the counseling, little Will would never leave his toys and drawings. He played contently. Even when there was deep hurt and pain being expressed, little Will would continue to play.

At one point when they were arguing and the argument turned to a power struggle that was going nowhere, little Will distracted the parents. I asked Will and Delores if they had noticed little Will's behavior. They immediately saw the connection between their behavior and little Will's. From then on they paid more attention to how their marital relationship affected little Will, and they sought to maintain appropriate conversation that allowed him to be himself and to play. They did not avoid conflict, but they handled the conflict without defensive power games that kept the anxiety up.

I was apprehensive about little Will's being in the counseling. However, I don't feel that the boundaries were blurred, because our focus was on their personal and marital relationships. I did learn what many marriage and family counselors have been saying for years, that is, that the marital relationship is often the source of good or bad parenting. When the marital relationship is functioning and meeting sufficiently the needs of both spouses, the parenting is influenced in a positive way. The opposite is also true.

Strengthening of the marital relationship also prevents the development of negative personal mythologies by children. When children are drawn into marital pain by parents with the hope of relieving the marital pain, irrational role assignments begin. This means that the child takes on adult responsibility prematurely, and the result is that the child loses his or her childhood. The generational boundaries are blurred, and the child becomes part of a myth that some call the family myth of overgeneralization.[11] This myth views every member of the family by a restricted set of role expectations. In the case of little Will, he could easily have been locked in the role of family mediator and have permanently lost his childhood. However, Will's and Delores' realization of the appropriate mode of communication during arguments, as well as the appropriate age-related needs of little Will, prevented a negative pattern from developing.

There was some recognition that Will, as an adult, played the role of helper in his family of origin, and his doing so was also a source of friction in the family. However, the death of Sam made his immediate family his priority more than his family of origin.

Will's growth and development came after there were break-throughs in Delores' life; at least, this was the way it appeared to me. It seemed that Will had no problems with her being the pioneer in certain areas in their emotional lives. Will admitted that his support of Delores' ministry was a way of avoiding his own call. He read all the seminary books that she brought home, so he was exposed to the same intellectual stimuli. He said he was happy not to have to go to seminary himself. I think this was also the case with grieving and growing in pastoral counseling. He would observe and learn and then imitate. How-ever, as a result of the death of Sam and the subsequent pastoral counseling relationship, he has set his own goals for growth and learning. He has completed seminary, and they are serving a church together.

THE RE-AUTHORING PROCESS

In the re-authoring process, the problem that exists within the family is identified, verbalized, and explored for the purpose of gaining a picture of the problem. Most important in this process is the ideal-child image expectations each spouse brings to the marital relationship. It is important to help the family identify what those ideal child images are early in the family counseling.

I was not able to assess the ideal child image that Delores and Will had with regard to Sam. However, his given name and his middle name were shared by biblical characters, and exploring the naming process might have revealed some of the ideal child expectations his parents had of him. Bagarozzi and Anderson outline some questions that can be raised that may elicit ideal child expectations.[12] These questions involve exploring the feel-ings both spouses have about the discovery of a pregnancy. The concerns are the following: (1) whether or not the pregnancy was wanted and planned, (2) the circumstances surrounding the pregnancy, (3) the reactions of the parents to seeing the child for the first time, (4) the grandparents' reaction to the pregnancy and birth, and the reactions of children to the birth, (5) the naming process, (6) the expectations about the child's behavior, (7) the values and ideas about child development, and (8) the contribution of the child to the family. The purpose of the questions is to ascertain whether or not there is some expectation that the child serve some purpose in the family that might hinder the growth and development of the child.

Sometimes the family interaction will reveal patterns related to ideal child expectations. For example, Delores and Will would argue in such a way that little Will would disrupt the counseling. In this way he was learning to be the mediator in marital conflict. If this pattern had not been interrupted, then one could have concluded that the family's ideal child role would be to intervene when parents cannot get along.

Re-authoring also involves finding unique possibilities that exist within the identified problem. Both Will and Delores found meaning in the midst of tragedy. They faced the problem together and grew as a result. They discovered their priorities and pursued them in responsible and emotionally healthy ways.

ROLE-TAKING, CONTINUITY, AND CHANGE

Role-taking with Bible characters and stories was instrumental in facilitating growth in the lives of Delores and Will. Like many of the other people in the cases presented, they also had been reared in churches where role-taking with Bible stories and characters was an important means of approaching experience. Role-taking was part of the lives of Delores and Will much the same way it was in the lives of the other persons presented in this book. Rather than illustrate how role-taking was involved in Delores and Will's life by covering ground already traversed, I would like to explore another dimension of role-taking that has not been introduced into the discussion. This relates to what H. Richard Niebuhr calls external history and inner history.

According to Niebuhr, external or outer history is God's self-manifestation and activity as revealed in Scripture and in the history of faith communities. Inner history begins when God's self-revelation and work affect a particular life and community, and the person and community become participants in God's external history.[13] When an individual encounters God's external history and decides to become a participant in it, metanoia or conversion takes place. In Niebuhr's view, a revolution takes place in one's whole life and mind. This decision to participate in God's external history constitutes a leap of faith where one begins to give the self over to God's salvation history. One result of this leap of faith is a different construal of time. One begins to look at the past, present, and future differently.[14]

Time can be divided into the past, present, and future. When one becomes a participant in God's external history, the failure to use past opportunities for fulfillment, which have been lost because of poorly made decisions, can be forgiven. One is released from the guilt for not actualizing certain choices that would have made a significant difference. One is not only released from past guilt, one is also liberated for the present and can take full advantage of the opportunities that come as a result, making external history inner history. Even more, the person faces the future with a hopeful faith that opportunities for fulfillment will be extended, because of God's faithfulness in carrying out God's purposes. Role-taking with Scripture is one of the principal ways outer history can become inner history in an individual's life.

Role-taking with specific Bible characters and stories continued to initiate Delores and Will into God's external history. The external history of God became their inner history. One result of their participation in God's history as their inner history was the slow transformation of the past and the release from tremendous guilt. They began to feel the release from the burden of guilt, which could not be overcome in their lives without participation in God's history. When they began to experience this release, they were able to turn their lives to the present and the opportunities that God was presenting them to fulfill their lives. Now, they not only take advantage of God's new opportunities for fulfillment, they also look to the future with hope.

It must be emphasized that Delores and Will's transformation took about four years. It was not a sudden event. It was a slow and painful process. It was much like an unfolding story that eventually reached the last chapter.

Both Delores and Will, as is true of the other people in the cases presented, were in an unfolding drama leading them toward wholeness, reconciliation, and improved relationships. Scripture in conjunction with pastoral counseling helped direct and support this unfolding drama.

CHAPTER SIX

THE BIBLE IN PASTORAL THEOLOGY

This book has sought to explore in detail the way counselees have storied their experiences in light of faith narratives from the Judeo-Christian tradition. In this effort resources from several different disciplines have been employed. These disciplines include biblical narrative criticism, the psychological and interpersonal theory of mythology, the psychology of shame and of object relations, counseling psychology, cultural analysis of shame and entitlement, role-taking theory, and pastoral theological method. Attention has been given to the cultural and secular stories that affect the way people story experience, and how faith stories challenge negative stories and support positive stories that affect the growth of persons.

Relating these diverse theoretical and theological areas requires a sophisticated pastoral theological method. Such a method must be open to communicating across different disciplines. It must relate theology and the behavioral sciences as well as biblical narrative criticism. It must also be adept at relating confessional dimensions of a faith community's theology with nontheological and secular disciplines. This pastoral theological model must also keep in focus the practical aspects of the ministry of pastoral care and counseling at the same time it relates theological and behavioral science disciplines. In brief, this model must be comprehensive theologically and theoretically while addressing specific practical situations.

The best practical theological method for handling this comprehensive task is the hermeneutics of engagement. The hermeneutics of engagement has four basic thrusts—a historical thrust, a contemporary thrust, an assessment thrust, and a practical thrust.[1]

The historical thrust of the method is akin to what H. Richard Niebuhr calls outer or external history.[2] External history is observation of God's activity in the past as it has been revealed in Scripture and in church history. The method of observation is biblical criticism. In this book, narrative biblical criticism has been the method for observing external history and God's activity in it. It was used to observe patterns of God's activity in the past, especially in the lives of people and in the lives of communities of faith. Such observations became the basis for understanding how God's activity manifests itself today.

The contemporary thrust of the hermeneutics of engagement is akin to what Niebuhr calls inner history. Outer history becomes inner history when a person or a community encounters God's unfolding and continuing outer history in the present. The person and community of faith move from observers of history to participants in history. Role-taking theory is utilized to understand how external history becomes inner history in the present. It is primarily through role-taking that one encounters the past in the present.

The third thrust of the hermeneutics of engagement involves exploring in depth how full participation in inner history affects the life of the participant. This is done through the use of behavioral science theories as analytical tools for examining the emotional and psychological difficulties people face. The psychology of mythology, object relations theory, and role-taking theory are examples of such analytical tools. Through such assessment devices it is possible to determine the influence of inner history on the growth and development of persons.

Once the impact on the inner history is determined, pastoral counseling is employed to assist inner history in its impact on the counselee. This addresses the practical side of the hermeneutics of engagement. This practical side is the fourth thrust of the hermeneutics of engagement.

In bringing this book to a close, it is crucial to lift up several pastoral theological issues related to the hermeneutics of engagement. These issues include (1) the relationship of revelation and reason, (2) the relationship of confessional pastoral theology and apologetic pastoral theology, (3) the hermeneutics of engagement and older correlational methods of pastoral theology, (4) the context of pastoral theology, and (5) the place of cultural issues in pastoral theology.

REASON AND REVELATION

The hermeneutics of engagement utilizes both story rational thinking and technical rational thinking. Story rational thinking is related to the imaginative, intuitive, and the "being grasped" aspect of thinking, while technical rational thinking refers to the more abstract, linear, and conceptual logic. For the purposes here, story rationality is related to revelation, and technical rationality is related to reason.

In historical Christian doctrine, the concern for faith and reason focused on how knowledge of God and of faith is achieved.[3] Traditionally, revelation had to do with God's self-disclosure in history and God's redemptive salvation activity. The question that is posed is whether knowledge of God and God's activity can be proved by reason or has to be accepted on faith.

In this book emphasis is given to historical and contemporary revelation. That is to say, the concern has been for how the Bible story (historical revelation) was at work at the depths of the person's life (contemporary revelation) to bring about change. The book has not proved that God is at work historically or contemporarily. The book has assumed this, because of my own participation in the faith tradition that has been explored. However, technical reason was not excluded. I have emphasized that storying experience is a form of rational knowing that is different from technical knowing. This builds on Paul Tillich's emphasis that there is revelational reason and technical reason.[4] Reason is involved in revelation. However, I have given priority to story reasoning, and I have used technical reasoning to derive further meaning from faith-storying. The re-authoring phase of pastoral counseling has been the phase in which technical reasoning is used to understand and explore the implications of the storying process.

CONFESSIONAL PASTORAL THEOLOGY AND APOLOGETIC PASTORAL THEOLOGY

Another issue that the hermeneutics of engagement raises is in the area of confessional theology versus apologetic theology. Confessional theology chooses as its starting point historical Christian revelation (outer history) and its faith stories and seeks to speak to the church in the categories of Christian faith and Christian revelation. Apologetic theology seeks to make Christian revelation meaningful to those outside the church by employing categories that come from contemporary culture. In other words, apologetic theology seeks to interpret Christian revelation in light of the categories of secular philosophy and the prevalent sciences and social sciences of contemporary life.

Christian apologetics has been an effort to defend the faith to what Deotis Roberts calls "the cultural despisers of the faith."[5] The apologists are acquainted with the literature, sciences, and philosophy of their day and seek to interpret the faith to the educated and literate.

It is quite clear that the hermeneutics of engagement has its apologetic aspects. It draws on the literature of psychology, counseling psychology, and marriage and family counseling theories that permeate the professions of counseling and psychotherapy. The hermeneutics of engagement as employed in this book speaks to those who are already within the confessional tradition. This work has sought to explore the use of Bible stories in the pastoral counseling process drawing insights from secular disciplines. The book has not attempted to address the secular audience in an apologetic way.

HERMENEUTICS OF ENGAGEMENT AND CORRELATIONAL METHODS

Within the history of contemporary pastoral theology, there have been several models. All of these models are a form of correlation used for relating theology and psychology. Seward Hiltner drew on Paul Tillich's correlational method in pastoral theology in his book *Preface to Pastoral Theology.*[6] He brought the shepherding perspective of the confessional faith tradition to bear on the practice of ministry and raised theological questions and derived theological answers.

The next model to emerge was Charles Gerkin's hermeneutical model in his book *The Living Human Document: Pastoral Counseling in a Hermeneutical Mode.*[7] In it he is concerned about how persons within the confessional tradition interpret and reinterpret themselves within the counseling process using the Judeo-Christian faith story. Donald Capps has joined Gerkin in exploring the hermeneutical dimensions of pastoral counseling.

The difference between traditional correlation and hermeneutics of engagement is in the use of tradition. In traditional correlation, faith tradition and secular disciplines are co-partners with both having equal status. The apologetic form of pastoral theology benefits more from traditional correlations. In hermeneutics of engagement the confessional tradition is given more of a central place.

The apologetic dimension of pastoral theology has benefited also by a new method called revised critical correlation. Don Browning builds on the work of David Tracy and develops this method in several books.[8] This method recognizes that the secular disciplines seek to answer ultimate questions of theology and ethics which have traditionally been the domain of theology. This revised critical correlation indicates that the areas of correspondence between the behavioral sciences and theology need to be attended to. Some pastoral theologians say that there is no real difference between the language of theology and the language of psychology. Browning does not make this conclusion, however.

In this book, I have used the hermeneutics of engagement. I believe that this model best facilitates doing confessional pastoral theology because it gives priority to the faith story in the dialogue between theology and the secular behavioral sciences. My concern is to use the behavioral and social sciences in the service of the faith confession. I do not envisage the social and behavioral sciences as equal partners with theology.

THE CONTEXT OF PASTORAL THEOLOGY

The hermeneutics of engagement takes more than the pastoral counseling setting seriously. The pastoral counseling relationship is only one arena where theological reflection takes place.

The context of church life and worship must be taken into account when doing confessional pastoral theology. These are settings where people encounter the faith story and reinforce the faith story. The parish context and the pastoral counseling context facilitate confessional pastoral theology. In the hermeneutics of engagement, pastoral counseling becomes an extension of the worshiping life of the church and of the pastoral counseling center. These contexts mutually influence each other and also influence the use of Bible stories in the life of the counselee.

In the secular setting the faith story must compete with other compelling stories. The reality of other professionals who see themselves differently from pastoral counselors enters into the dynamics in pastoral care and counseling. It is difficult for worship and congregational life to influence the counselee in a secular setting.

In this book both the counselees and the pastoral counselor have viewed themselves as part of the ministry of the church. The pastoral counseling took place in a pastoral counseling center that envisaged itself as part of the church and the church's ministry.

CULTURAL ISSUES AND PASTORAL THEOLOGY

It is not possible to do pastoral theological reflection without addressing cultural issues. People bring in the prevalent cultural issues that affect their lives. This is particularly the case in personal, marital, and family mythologies. These mythologies have their cultural components. They are reinforced by cultural processes that are at work.

The hermeneutics of engagement does not ignore these wider cultural issues as they emerge. It draws cultural dimensions into the process of pastoral counseling and into pastoral theology.

IN CONCLUSION

This book has used the hermeneutics of engagement to illustrate the use of Bible stories in pastoral counseling. This method and the model of using the Bible in pastoral counseling have shown that the Bible can be used in pastoral counseling. This is particularly the case with persons who have a role-taking history with the Bible.

Although I have found Bible stories useful and helpful for the people with whom I have worked, there are some real limitations to this method. One of the limitations is that not all counselees come from biblically rich backgrounds. These persons could benefit greatly from the use of Bible stories if appropriate methods for making the stories accessible to them existed. Methods of making Scripture relevant for such persons need more attention.

Another limitation of the book is that the counselees in the case studies were all African American. Though this was a limited sample, I have worked with counselees and students who were white, Hispanic, and Asian. The same principles in the book also apply to these non–African American persons, especially if they come from Bible-rich churches. However, further exploration in this area is needed to follow up on the usefulness of this method for non–African American persons.

A third limitation of the book is that there are those who suffer from extremely frustrating relationships in their lives. Their use of stories is often distorted and twisted. Sometimes, such persons want to identify with negative biblical stories and characters. Or the people who have relayed Bible stories and ideas to them may have distorted them as a result of their own frustrations or lack of comprehension. In these circumstances this method can be modified to help persons to choose stories and characters that challenge old negative Bible identifications and that facilitate their growth. For an example of how this is done, see *Prayer in Pastoral Counseling: Suffering, Healing, and Discernment.*[9]

I recognize that Bible stories are often problematic for many groups of people including many women. I am continually fascinated by women who still find positive stories within the Scripture with which to identify as a means of growth. Because the Bible has played such a favorable role in the lives of many

African American women, I have learned from them that there are liberating stories and traditions within the Bible that can facilitate the growth of all persons. In addition, some women who are biblical scholars, like Phyllis Bird, a former colleague at Garrett-Evangelical, are helping to call attention to these stories and traditions.

Because the Bible is making a return in many churches as an authoritative document, effort needs to be made to make sure that pastors and laypersons learn to use Bible stories in ways that facilitate growth. I have made some suggestions in this book about how this can be done in pastoral counseling. I know of similar efforts being made in Christian education, and in preaching. Study guides for Bible studies are also appearing that take seriously the use of growth-facilitating stories in the life of the church. Yet much more work needs to be done to help appropriate the growth-facilitating stories of the Bible for the growth of persons.

NOTES

PREFACE

1. Edward P. Wimberly, *African American Pastoral Care* (Nashville: Abingdon Press, 1991).

CHAPTER 1: A MODEL FOR USING SCRIPTURE IN PASTORAL COUNSELING

1. Dennis A. Bagarozzi and Stephen A. Anderson, *Personal, Marital, and Family Myths* (New York: W. W. Norton and Co., 1989), 15.
2. Many of the ideas for this section are found in Bagarozzi and Anderson, *Personal, Marital, and Family Myths*, 28-41.
3. Michael White and David Epston, in *Narrative Means to Therapeutic Ends* (New York: W. W. Norton and Co., 1990), provide a significant vocabulary for those who want to delve further into the theory of editing personal mythologies.
4. For a discussion of role-taking theory, see Nils G. Holm, "Sunden's Role Theory and Glosso-lalia," *Journal for the Scientific Study of Religion* 26 (1987): 383-89; Donald Capps, "Sunden's Role-Taking: The Case of John Henry Newman and His Mentors," *Journal for the Scientific Study of Religion* 21 (1982): 58-70; Thorvald Kallstad, "The Application of the Religio-Psychological Role Theory," *Journal for the Scientific Study of Religion* 26 (1987): 367-74; and Hjalmar Sunden, "Saint Augustine and the Psalter in the Light of Role Theory," *Journal for the Scientific Study of Religion* 26 (1987): 375-82.
5. See Robert C. Tannehill, *The Narrative Unity of Luke-Acts: A Literary Interpretation* (Philadelphia: Fortress Press, 1986), 8.
6. Kallstad, "Application of the Role Theory," 368.
7. For a study of the use of narrative criticism in biblical studies, see Mark A. Powell, *What Is Narrative Criticism* (Minneapolis: Fortress Press, 1990).
8. See Bagarozzi and Anderson, *Personal, Marital, and Family Myths*.
9. Ibid., 78.
10. Ibid., 206-98.
11. See Donald Capps, "Bible, Pastoral Use and Interpretation of," *Dictionary of Pastoral Care and Counseling*, Rodney Hunter, ed. (Nashville: Abingdon Press, 1990), 82-85.

Chapter 2: Personal Mythology and Bible Stories

1. For a discussion of alternation, see Nils G. Holm, "Sunden's Role Theory and Glossolalia," *Journal for the Scientific Study of Religion* 26 (1987): 384.
2. Robert C. Tannehill, *The Narrative Unity of Luke-Acts* (Philadelphia: Fortress Press, 1986), 90.
3. Ibid., 7.
4. Ibid., 91.
5. Ibid.
6. Ibid., 92.
7. Ibid.
8. Ibid., 96.
9. For additional references for definitions and descriptions of the narrator, see Seymour Chatman, *Story and Discourse: Narrative Structure in Fiction and Film* (Ithaca, N.Y.: Cornell University Press, 1978), 147-51; and Mikeal C. Parsons, "Reading a Beginning/Beginning a Reading: Tracking Literary Theory on Narrative Openings," *Semeia: An Experimental Journal for Biblical Criticism* 52 (1990): 19-21.
10. Paul Ricoeur, *Symbolism of Evil* (Boston: Beacon Press, 1967), 352.
11. For simultaneous role-taking, see Donald Capps, "Sunden's Role-Taking: The Case of John Henry Newman and His Mentors," *Journal for the Scientific Study of Religion* 21 (1982): 59.
12. For the function of entitlement in our society and its origin in our early childhood relationships, see Marion Solomon, *Narcissism and Intimacy, Love and Marriage in the Age of Confusion* (New York: W. W. Norton, 1989), 9-12.
13. See John Bradshaw, *Healing the Shame That Binds You* (Dearfield Beach, Fla.: Health Communications, 1988), 115-16.
14. Leon Wurmser, *The Mask of Shame* (Baltimore: Johns Hopkins University Press, 1981), 49-50, 92-93.
15. Embarrassment is associated with shame. See James Harper and Margaret Hoopes, *Uncovering Shame* (New York: W. W. Norton, 1990), 8.
16. The 12-step recovery programs were made famous by Alcoholics Anonymous.
17. James Limburg, *Interpretation: A Bible Commentary for Teaching and Preaching Hosea-Micah* (Atlanta: John Knox Press, 1988), 156.
18. Ibid., 152.
19. Douglas Stuart, *Word Biblical Commentary: Hosea-Jonah* (Waco: Word Books, 1987), 435-36.

Chapter 3: Personal Mythology and Abuse

1. Christie Cozad Neuger, "Women's Depression: Lives at Risk," in *Women in Travail and Transition: A New Pastoral Care*, Maxine Glaz and Jeanne Stevenson Moessner, eds. (Minneapolis: Fortress Press, 1991), 155.
2. Nancy Ramsay, "Sexual Abuse and Shame: The Travail of Recovery," in *Women in Travail and Transition*, 119.
3. Ibid., 120.
4. Ibid., 109-25.
5. Ibid., 112.
6. Ibid., 113.

7. Ibid.

8. Ibid., 114.

9. Ibid.

10. JoAnne M. Garma, "A Cry of Anguish: Battered Woman," in *Women in Travail and Transition*, 126-45.

11. Neuger, "Women's Depression," 152-55.

12. Ibid., 158.

13. Claus Westermann, *The Living Psalms* (Grand Rapids: Wm. B. Eerdmans Publishing Co., 1984), vii.

14. Ibid., 1.

15. Ibid., 4-5.

16. Ibid., 11.

17. Ibid., 166.

18. Ibid., 190-96.

19. See William James, *Varieties of Religious Experience* (New York: Mentor Books, 1958), 191-92; and Wayne Oates, *Psychology and Religion* (Waco, Tex.: Word, 1973), 34.

CHAPTER 4: MARITAL MYTHOLOGY AND THE IDEAL MATE

1. Dennis A. Bagarozzi and Stephen A. Anderson, *Personal, Marital, and Family Myths* (New York: W. W. Norton and Co., 1989), 17.

2. Ibid., 77.

3. Ibid., 86-88.

4. Ibid., 87.

5. James M. Harper and Margaret H. Hoopes, *Uncovering Shame* (New York: W. W. Norton and Co., 1990), 89-91.

6. Ibid.

7. Ibid.

8. Ibid.

9. Carol H. Lankton and Stephen R. Lankton, *Tales of Enchantment* (New York: Brunner/Mazel, 1989), 27-31.

10. Terrence C. Fretheim, *Interpretation: A Bible Commentary for Teaching and Preaching Exodus* (Louisville: John Knox Press, 1991), 8.

11. Ibid., 18.

12. Ibid., 294.

13. Ibid., 171.

14. Ibid.

15. For a discussion of the possibility expectations, see Mary Ellen Oliveri and David Reiss, "Family Styles of Construing the Social Environment: A Perspective on Variation Among Nonclinical Families," in *Normal Family Process*, ed. Froma Walsh (New York: Guilford Press, 1982), 100-101.

CHAPTER 5: FAMILY MYTHOLOGY AND GRIEVING FOR A CHILD

1. Delores Johnson, "My Favorite Bible Text," *Gospel Herald and the Sunday School Times* (Spring Quarter, 1992), 52 (116). Reprinted by permission of the Incorporated Trustees of the Gospel Worker Society, Union Gospel Press, P.O. Box 6059, Cleveland, Ohio 44101.

2. Dennis A. Bagarozzi and Stephen A. Anderson, *Personal, Marital, and Family Myths* (New York: W. W. Norton and Co., 1989), 206-8.

3. See James Framo, "Symptoms from a Family Transactional Viewpoint" in *Progress in Group and Family Therapy*, H. S. Kaplan and C. J. Sager, eds. (New York: Brunner/Mazel, 1972), 273-74.

4. For the concepts of blurring boundaries, see Edward P. Wimberly, *Pastoral Counseling and Spiritual Values: A Black Point of View* (Nashville: Abingdon, 1982), 110-15.

5. James L. Mays, ed., *Harper's Bible Dictionary* (San Francisco: Harper and Row, 1988), 473-74.

6. Donald Capps, *Biblical Approaches to Pastoral Counseling* (Philadelphia: Westminster Press, 1981), 47-97.

7. Ibid., 75.

8. Ibid., 74.

9. Claus Westermann, *The Living Psalms* (Grand Rapids: Wm. B. Eerdmans Publishing Co., 1984), 128.

10. Mays, *Harper's Bible Dictionary*, 441.

11. See Vimala Pillari, *Pathways to Family Myths* (New York: Brunner/Mazel, 1986), 9-10.

12. Bagarozzi and Anderson, *Personal, Marital, and Family Myths*, 226-27.

13. See H. Richard Niebuhr, *The Meaning of Revelation* (New York: Macmillan, 1941), 59-66.

14. Thomas Oden explores the time dimensions of history in terms of past, present, and future. See *Structure of Awareness* (Nashville/New York: Abingdon Press, 1969), 13-20.

CHAPTER 6: THE BIBLE IN PASTORAL THEOLOGY

1. See Edward P. Wimberly and Anne E. Wimberly, *Liberation and Human Wholeness* (Nashville: Abingdon Press, 1986), 22.

2. H. Richard Niebuhr, *The Meaning of Revelation* (New York: Macmillan, 1941), 59-66.

3. J. Deotis Roberts, *A Philosophical Introduction to Theology* (Philadelphia: Trinity Press International, 1991), 111-12.

4. Paul Tillich, *Systematic Theology*, vol. 1 (Chicago: University of Chicago Press, 1951), 71-159.

5. Roberts, *A Philosophical Introduction*, 87.

6. Seward Hiltner, *Preface to Pastoral Theology* (Nashville/New York: Abingdon Press, 1958), 222-23.

7. Charles Gerkin, *The Living Human Document: Pastoral Counseling in a Hermeneutical Mode* (Nashville: Abingdon Press, 1986).

8. See Don Browning, *Religious Thought and the Modern Psychologies: A Critical Conversation in the Theology and Culture* (Philadelphia: Fortress Press, 1987), and *A Foundational Practical Theology* (Minneapolis: Fortress Press, 1991).

9. Edward P. Wimberly, *Prayer in Pastoral Counseling: Suffering, Healing, and Discernment* (Louisville: Westminster/John Knox Press, 1990).

BIBLIOGRAPHY

Adams, Jay. *Competent to Counsel*. Grand Rapids: Baker Books, 1970.

Bagarozzi, Dennis A., and Stephen A. Anderson. *Personal, Marital, and Family Myths*. New York: W. W. Norton and Co., 1989.

Barker, Philip. *Using Metaphors in Psychotherapy*. New York: Brunner/Mazel, 1985.

Bradshaw, John. *Healing the Shame That Binds You*. Dearfied Beach, Florida: Health Communications, 1988.

Browning, Don S. A *Fundamental Practical Theology*. Minneapolis: Fortress Press, 1991.

Brueggemann, Walter. *Hope Within History*. Atlanta: John Knox Press, 1987.

Capps, Donald. *Biblical Themes in Pastoral Counseling*. Philadelphia: Westminster Press, 1981.

———. "Sunden's Role-taking Theory: The Case of John Henry and His Mentors," *Journal for the Scientific Study of Religion* 21 (1982): 60.

———. *Reframing*. Minneapolis: Fortress Press, 1991.

Chapman, Thomas, ed. *Practical Handbook for Ministry: From the Writings of Wayne E. Oates*. Louisville: Westminster/John Knox Press, 1992.

Chatman, Seymour. *Story and Discourse: Narrative Structure in Fiction and Film*. Ithaca, N.Y.: Cornell University, 1978.

Clinebell, Howard J. *Basic Types of Pastoral Care and Counseling*. Nashville: Abingdon Press, 1984.

Felder, Cain Hope, ed. *Stoney the Road We Trod: African American Biblical Interpretation*. Minneapolis: Fortress Press, 1991.

———. *Troubling Biblical Waters: Race, Class, and Family*. Maryknoll, N.Y.: Orbis Books, 1989.

Garma, JoAnne M. "A Cry of Anguish: Battered Women," in *Women in Travail and Transition: A New Pastoral Care*, ed. Maxine Glaz and Jeanne Stevenson Moessner. Minneapolis: Fortress Press, 1991.

Gerkin, Charles. *The Living Human Document: Pastoral Counseling in a Hermeneutical Mode*. Nashville: Abingdon Press, 1986.

Harper, James, and Margaret Hoopes. *Uncovering Shame*. New York: W. W. Norton and Co., 1990.

Hopewell, James. *Congregations, Stories, and Structures*. Philadelphia: Fortress Press, 1987.

Hunter, Rodney, ed. *Dictionary of Pastoral Care and Counseling*. Nashville: Abingdon Press, 1990.

Johnson, Delores. "My Favorite Bible Text," *Gospel Herald and the Sunday School Times* (Spring Quarter, 1989).

Jordan, Merle R. *Taking on the gods: The Task of the Pastoral Counselor*. Nashville: Abingdon Press, 1986.

Kallstad, Thorvald. "The Application of the Religio-Psychological Role Theory," *Journal for the Scientific Study of Religion* 26 (1987): 367-74.

Lankton, Carol H., and Stephen R. Lankton. *Tales of Enchantment*. New York: Brunner/Mazel, 1989.

Limburg, James. *Interpretation: A Bible Commentary for Teaching and Preaching*. Atlanta: John Knox Press, 1988.

Neuger, Christie Cozad. "Women's Depression: Lives at Risk," in *Women in Travail and Transition: A New Pastoral Care*, ed. Maxine Glaz and Jeanne Stevenson Moessner. Minneapolis: Fortress Press, 1991.

Niebuhr, H. Richard. *The Meaning of Revelation*. New York: Macmillan, 1941.

Oates, Wayne. *The Bible in Pastoral Care*. Philadelphia: Westminster Press, 1953.

Oglesby, William B. *Biblical Themes in Pastoral Care*. Nashville: Abingdon, 1980.

Patton, John. *Is Human Forgiveness Possible?* Nashville: Abingdon Press, 1985.

Powell, Mark. *What Is Narrative Criticism?* Minneapolis: Augsburg Fortress, 1990.

Ramsay, Nancy. "Sexual Abuse and Shame: The Travail of Recovery," in *Women in Travail and Transition: A New Pastoral Care*, ed. Maxine Glaz and Jeanne Stevenson Moessner. Minneapolis: Fortress Press, 1991.

Ricoeur, Paul. *Symbolism of Evil*. Boston: Beacon Press, 1967.

Tannehill, Robert C. *The Narrative Unity of Luke-Acts*. Philadelphia: Fortress Press, 1986.

Vitz, Paul. "Narrative and Counseling, Part I: From Analysis of the Past to Stories About It," *Journal of Psychology and Theology* 20 (1992): 11-19.